The

SURREY Weather Book

A Century of Storms, Floods and Freezes

by Mark Davison and Ian Currie

It was Samuel Johnson who wrote, 'When two Englishmen meet, their first talk is of the weather'. The recent past has provided Surrey's residents with more than enough to chat about. Twice in one year the working day ground to a halt when, in 1987, snowstorms and then hurricane force winds closed schools, shops and offices. Global warming or not, there then followed droughts, further winter gales and remarkable heatwaves that led to water restrictions and raging heathland fires. But the extreme heat of 1989 and 1990 was a boost to Surrey's vineyards.

Things may be happening fast and furious in the weather world at present, but floods and freezes, hailstorms and tempests have always been part and parcel of our climate.

This book is a pictorial record of some of those atmospheric occasions when owing to the inclement weather, the train that should have arrived on platform two really was buried in a snowdrift. And when grandad spoke of paddling along the High Street in a canoe, he certainly was telling the truth.

FROSTED EARTH

Point duty at East Clandon in the January 1987 blizzards.

ISBN 0-9516710-1-4

First edition November 1990
Second revised edition October 1991

Published by Frosted Earth,
77 Rickman Hill, Coulsdon,
Surrey CR5 3DT
Tel: 0737 554869

Typeset by ***White Art, Whyteleafe.***

Printed by ***Litho Techniques, Kenley.***

Acknowledgements

John Janaway, Surrey Local Studies Library, Guildford; Kingston Heritage Centre; Surrey Comet; Farnham Herald; Farnham Library; Elmbridge Museum; Elmbridge Council; Croydon Natural History and Scientific Society; Climatological Observers Link; Surrey Mirror; Epsom and Sutton Herald Series; Guildford Library; Surrey County Council; Surrey Herald; Croydon Advertiser; W. Harvey, Ewell; Jane Pearce, Woking; Woking News and Mail; Jack Sales, Redhill; Weather Magazine; Royal Meteorological Society; Surrey Fire Brigade; Stn. Off. Rodliff; Sandra Heath; Chobham Fire Station; Leading Fireman Belcher; Alan Greenwood, Chobham; Kingfield Conservation Group, M. and N. Davison, Hook; Keith Walter; J. Currie; Ben Murray; John Bradbury; Gaye Wilkinson, Brockham; Kingston Borough News; Lee Edgson; Tim Everson, Kingston; Colin Cornish, Kingston; Surrey Police; Neil McGinn; John Elms; Croydon Library; Hook Library; Surrey Advertiser; Evelyn Gillen; Peter Gardner; A. Cattermole; David Tippet-Wilson; Jean Moore, Hook; Doris Cook, Bletchingley; Camberley News; Dorking Advertiser; Leatherhead Advertiser; East Grinstead Observer; Ben Devlin; Barbara Macdonald; Mike Beardall; Sue Medland, East Surrey Water plc; Ruth Ledwich, Epsom Downs.

Photograph Credits

1894-5 winter: Kingston Heritage Centre; Surrey Local Studies Library, Guildford, late Rowland Baker. Lightning at Oxted: Guy Walkden. 1927-8 snow and floods: Jack Sales (Godstone vet and Tilburstow Hill drifts); Mrs Doris Geary and Tatsfield villagers (snow scenes at Tatsfield); O.S. Illman (snow gang on downs), Gerald Jenkins (Reigate Hill men). 1938 snow scene: Jack Sales. Winter of 1947: Jack Sales; D.T. Richardson, Oxted (Cudham bus). 1950 April snow: Farnham Herald. 1963 winter: Ron Poore (Chelsham snow scenes); Surrey Mirror (Earlswood Lakes and helicopter); Elmbridge Museum and Thorn and Mays (frozen Thames). Wisley tornado, 1965: The RHS Gardens Club Journal. 1968 floods: Mrs Perry (Stamford Green scenes); Surrey Comet (Army aid, Downside Bridge, Molesey boat rescue); Mr F. Gregory and Elmbridge Museum (Hersham floods); Surrey Local Studies Library, Guildford (Guildford shops flood); South East London Mercury (West Croydon-bound bus). The Times (submerged phone box); Mr George Lavender (Oxted scenes). Hook cloudburst 1973: Mr Webber, Hook. Heatwave 1976: Farnham Herald (cows at Thursley, fire Tilford); Thames Water plc (Walton reservoir); Tony Hines (dried up River Mole). Darkness at midday, 1981: Mr Vic Dowdeswell (Lower Kingswood scene); Croydon Advertiser (Croydon shops flooded). 1978 snow at Hook: Mark Davison. 1981 cold spell: Peter Gardner, Dorking Advertiser. March 1987 storm: Surrey Mirror. January 1987 snow: Camberley News (church fire); Banstead Herald (Banstead High Street); Ian Currie (Rickman Hill and Reigate Hill); Jon Russell (Titsey Hill). October 1987 Great Storm: Philip Holloway (Dorking sign). Great Gale 1990: Surrey Herald and Surrey Comet. August 1990 heatwave; Alan Greenwood collection (old fire engine and Horsell Common); Sandra Heath, Surrey Fire Brigade (Ash Ranges fire); Mark Davison (Tilford children and Kingfield Pond); Leatherhead Advertiser (grapevine); Joan Jones (West End Pond). February 1991 freeze up; Epsom and Sutton Heralds, Dorking Advertiser, Ann Cattermole, Bob Heron, Mark Davison, Ian Currie. Summer 1991 thunderstorm; Croydon Advertiser. Author pictures; Croydon Advertiser and Bob Heron.

A special thanks to Peter Clarke, Surrey Comet weather columnist 1970-1985.

Front cover: *Travelling problems on the Farnham Road just outside Guildford on 28th December 1927. Picture by D. Box, courtesy of Surrey Local Studies Library, Guildford.*

Back cover: *Top picture – The destruction of the old bridge at Guildford, on 16th February 1900 after rapidly melting snow and rain turned the River Wey into a raging torrent. One arch collapsed after tons of timber were swept downstream. Courtesy of Surrey Local Studies Library. Bottom picture – Downside Bridge at Cobham in the September 1968 floods. Courtesy of Surrey Comet.*

Logo: *Cathie Shuttleworth.*

Bibliography

Surrey in the Hurricane by Davison and Currie, published by Froglets.

London's Hurricane by Davison and Currie, published by Froglets.

The Weather of Britain by Robin Sterling, published by Faber and Faber.

London Weather by J.H. Brazell, published by H.M.S.O.

British Weather Disasters by Ingrid Holford, published by David and Charles.

Environmental Hazards in the British Isles by A.H. Perry, published by George Allen & Unwin.

The Rainfall of the British Isles by M de Carle, S. Salter published by University of London Press Ltd.

The A25 Nutfield to Bletchingley road after the great Boxing Day blizzard of 1927.

Snow piled deep in Claremont Road, Surbiton, soon after trams were introduced in 1906.

Skating On The Ponds 1878-9

By November 1878, the weather had turned decidedly cold, heralding three months of bitter conditions interrupted only by a few brief mild interludes.

The icy conditions well and truly set in early in December and on 11 days snow fell. In the parks around Richmond and Kingston skating became a favourite past-time from mid December.

Before Christmas many people cautiously stepped on to the ice but in places it was not strong enough to support the weight of human beings and some of them vanished into the icy water before being rescued. Warnings were put up but these were often ignored.

Just before Christmas 1878, local weather watchers predicted a long spell of severe weather, and this proved to be prophetic. Heavy snow fell right across Surrey on 22nd December and a large number of workmen were summoned to clear Home Park near Hampton Court. Thousands of people turned to skating as the icy weather tightened its grip.

A white Christmas was experienced and families ventured out to the frozen lakes. In the Kingston area on Christmas Eve, the mercury plunged to 15F (-9C). That's 17 degrees of frost on our forefathers' scales.

Union workhouses throughout the district were reported to be filled to capacity and there was much concern about the drain on taxpayers' money.

Despite a thaw at the end of December 1878, which caused the Thames to burst its banks, the severe weather was back with a vengeance in January 1879, and snow fell on 15 days.

There have only been five colder winters than 1878/9 since 1659. Surrey suffered 16 months starting from October 1878 to February 1880 with below average temperatures, and persistent dullness.

The Great Victorian Blizzard

18th January 1881

Described as the worst gale and snowstorm in any living person's memory, this phenomenal blizzard certainly ranks as one of the most severe in Victorian times. Shops were forced to close, vehicles were completely buried and a train came off the tracks.

Such was the ferocity of the snowstorm that the Croydon Advertiser reported that it was 'the meteorological event of the nineteenth century.'

The scene in Croydon was indicative of the type of conditions experienced all over Surrey and South London, with everyday life in a busy town grinding to a halt.

Caught in the teeth of the savage gale, Croydon battled to keep the snow out of buildings, but the millions of tiny ice crystals driven by such a fantastic wind forced their way into homes and shops and piled up inside.

An enthusiastic reporter on the Croydon Advertiser described how 'a perfect hurricane blew from the east north-east and swept the snow about with boisterous fury.' The vivid account noted that 'it was not wet snow but small hard nuts of ice' and 'was driven with extraordinary violence against window panes awakening those in slumber.'

At the height of the storm, 'the opening of a street door was a work of ease, but the attempt to shut it operated as a signal to the wind which threw its whole fury into the balance against the muscular powers of the door-closer, and when human power prevailed against it, the wind seemed to shriek out a wild cry of bitter anger and disappointed fury.'

Throughout the town, shops had to close as the blizzard raged on. At Croydon General Post Office, the glass doors could not be kept closed and the snow burst in and 'careered around the clerks who stood top-coated at the counter endeavouring to persuade their cold and aching fingers to write.' The Post Office floor and counter were covered in a mantle of white and the snow even penetrated into the sorting and telegraphic offices at the rear 'with remarkable and exasperating perseverance.'

At Smitham Bottom, near Purley, a van belonging to Mr R. F. Holloway, a Wallington bedding manufacturer was caught in the drifts. It was so deeply buried that three men dug for some time until any part of the vehicle could be seen. In Croydon, cabbies charged 'fancy prices' for travel. The railways came to a standstill and it took nearly three hours to get from Croydon to London. At Streatham, the last train from Victoria got snowed in and had to be dug out, and at Norwood, there were reports that the roof of the Norwood Junction Station had been blown off. Furthermore, a train carrying a few passengers came off the rails in the cutting between Kenley and Caterham Junction.

Back in Croydon, the northern door of the Town Hall could not be opened that night due to the threat of an invasion by snow. In Katherine Street at half past seven, one or two members of the School Board met at the offices but had to wait half an hour for the chairman to arrive to make up a quorum. It was learned that Dr. Roberts 'had been engaged in a hand-to-hand encounter with the elements for a considerable time while forcing his way from his place of residence in the south end of the High Street to the centre of the town.'

Croydon Theatre was closed on that wild and wintry night because snow had got into the dressing rooms. Mr Stanton, who ran the theatre, gave his company a night off.

The next day, cabs linked to two horses overcame the deep snow, but double fares were charged.

Skating was reported on many lakes in and around Surrey, including those at South Norwood, Merlands Park, Wellesley House, Cavan Villa, Crystal Palace Waters, Princess Road, Mitcham and Carshalton.

The cause of the snowstorm was a deep low pressure system which joined a battle between warmer Atlantic air and bitterly cold continental air. Winds reached gale force and gusted to more than 60 mph, causing considerable wind chill to anybody venturing out of doors.

Ice floes on the River Thames at Putney in January 1881.

The Thames In Flood

November 1894

Very heavy rain which fell during November 1894 brought terrible flooding to low-lying Surrey as the River Thames burst its banks and washed through shops and houses in Chertsey, Molesey and Kingston.

In early November, the level of the river was alarmingly high but as the late autumn rains continued to lash down from the murky skies, anxious householders became increasingly worried. In the Grove Road area of Chertsey on 18th November, people woke up to find 'furniture and effects' merrily floating around the room 'to music supplied by the in-flowing waters.'

The Surrey Herald on 24th November stated: 'In Guildford Street it first came into the road on Saturday morning, issuing with great force through the gates of Cowley House, across the road and path, and finally emptying itself into the Bourne on the opposite side of the road.'

In Bridge Road, Chertsey, the water 'was washing through the houses with the greatest of licence and as the day wore on, the waters rose and carts were fetched out to do duty as conveyances for the use of the public. Horses were made to shamble through the rushing waters, drop their burdens at one end, only to take up fresh ones and return, at the very moderate rate of a penny a ride.'

By 6 p.m. the water was running several inches deep over the Guildford Street paths, whilst in some parts of the road it was a foot deep or more. From the further end of Chapel Lane in Windsor Street, right along to St Ann's Road, Grove Road, Masonic Hall Road and St Ann's Grove, the waters rose. Two punts were continually at work carrying people to and from their dwellings, entrance to which was generally obtained by means of chairs placed from the punts to the bottom of the staircases.

The Herald noted, 'On Saturday evening the usual concourse of people came into the town by rail to do their shopping, and their numbers were augmented by those who came out of pure curiosity. Upon the temporary platform in Guildford Street, the weight was so great that the planks gave way and a number of people dropped into the water up to their knees.'

For the shoppers of Molesey, punts were used to ferry people along Walton Road and in Kingston the High Street was several inches deep and boats were used to transport townsfolk along the road.

It was set against such a chaotic and waterlogged background that the next momentous weather event was to take place just eight weeks later. Intense cold descended on the district in January 1895 and the Thames, up until then an unruly river of muddy torrents, was transformed by a schizophrenic atmosphere into giant fields of ice that would be remembered for many years.

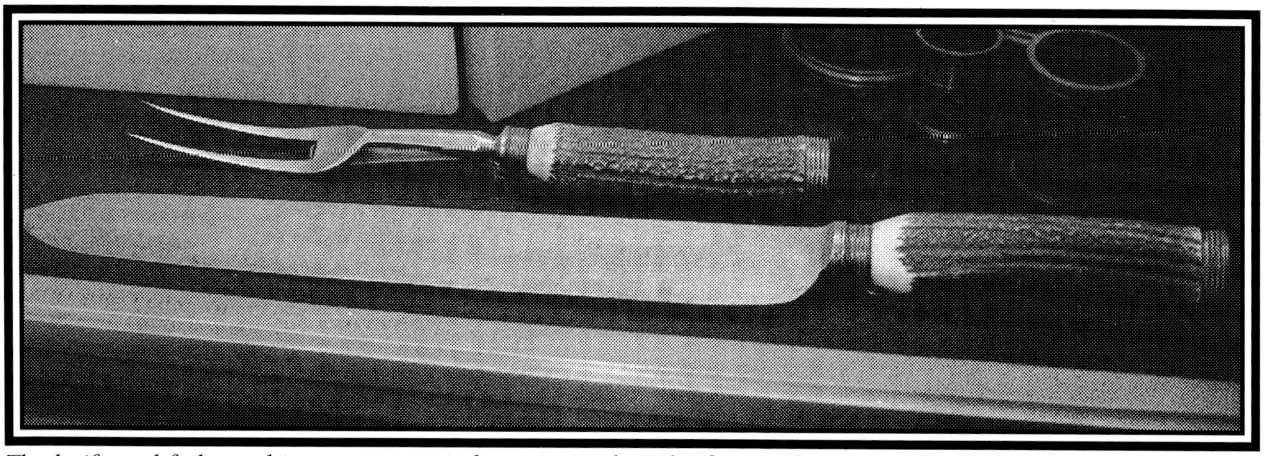

The knife and fork used to carve a roasted ox prepared on the frozen Thames in 1895. They are on display at the Kingston Heritage Centre.

On the night of 16th November 1894, the cry went up 'Take To The Boats' as the Thames burst its banks and swamped most of central Kingston. At the High Street (above), Kingston Corporation put down a few flimsy planks but taxi-boats had to be used to get down the road towards Surbiton.
Sightseers flocked to Kingston to view the spectacle and impromptu regattas were held. At first, boat-men 'charged fancy prices' to rescue people from their flooded homes, but when the free boat service was started up by the council, this enterprise stopped.
Behind the lighter moments there was much hardship and despair. Residents of the tenements in Eden Street, Brook Street and Wood Street could ill afford to pay for pumps to rid their simple dwellings of the sewage-laden waters.

Some Stories Grandfather Told

1703 The most damaging storm in history occurred in November - even worse than the so-called 'hurricane' of October 1987.

1728 A violent tempest unleashed massive hailstones over Croydon on 12th May which shattered windows and buildings. Cattle were drowned in ditches while trying to seek shelter. The huge chunks of ice punched holes in the ground several inches deep.

1814 A thick freezing fog on the 27th December 1813 was followed in early January by a 48 hour snowstorm. Esher and Cobham were completely blocked and the Newcastle coach came to grief as it careered off the road into an eight foot pit.

1818 A 'very uncommon summer for heat and duration'. Alarming shortage of water.

1826 Remarkably hot and dry summer. Wells and river dried up completely. 'Much distress on the hills from want of water.' Wheat crops abundant, but barley and oats very short. Peas totally lost.

1836 At Cobham on 29th October, an extraordinary snowfall covered the ground to a depth of several inches and lay for five days. October accumulations in Surrey are virtually unheard of in the 20th century.

1838 Possibly the coldest period of the last 200 years occurred in January. On 20th, Lady Caroline Molesworth recorded -10F (-23C) at Cobham, and Lady Moore's thermometer 'had no quicksilver to be seen' at 8 am.

1849 On the 19th April 1849 the Westerham coach was buried in a snowdrift on Titsey Hill and had to be left there all night.

1855 Hockey was played on the frozen Thames at Richmond during the icy cold February.

1867 It was reported that a temperature as low as -12F (-24C) was measured at Epsom early on the 4th January 1867. Three days later the mercury reached 54F (12C).

1878-9 Cold and snowy winter with lakes and ponds frozen over.

1880 On 20th October the sheer weight of snow on trees damaged many oaks and elms. Boughs up to 30 feet long were torn down. Weybridge was particularly hit.

1881 Great blizzard on 18th January. Vehicles completely buried outside Croydon.

1882 On 29th April 'a great mischief' was done to tree blossom by salt blown in from the sea by a severe gale. 'Flowers were completely stripped off and the leaves lashed by the fury of the wind into shreds and turning quite black, as if withered by a sharp frost.'

1888 During the dismal, very cool wet summer, snow was reported to have fallen at Norwood on the 11th July.

1890 December was the coldest for 150 years, and desperately bleak. Richmond only had 20 minutes' sunshine all month. The average amount is around 43 hours.

1891 A snowstorm commenced on March 9th which rivalled January 1881. A man was found dead in the snow near Dorking and a train had to be abandoned close to Croydon. Further snow fell in May.

1894-5 Disastrous floods in November followed by severe cold later in the winter. On 8th February, the temperature at Beddington near Croydon plummeted to -2F (-19C).

Shoppers had to go out in punts to bring in the provisions after the Thames burst its banks in November 1894 and flooded Walton Road, East Molesey (above and right).

FROM 23rd October to 17th November 1894, more than 8 ins (200mm) of rain fell in the Thames Valley – almost a third of the normal annual rainfall.

It is estimated that 600 families had to live in the upstairs rooms of their homes. At Eton, it was the worst flood since 1774 and at Windsor, the highest flood on record with water lapping four inches higher than a previous severe flood in 1852 which carried away the Duke of Wellington's hearse at Maidenhead.

Above: *Looking down Portsmouth Road, Kingston, towards the town centre during the floods of November 1894.*
Below: *Riverside dwellings near Kingston are completely marooned by the invading Thames.*

There was only one way to get down Lower Ham Road, Kingston, in the 1894/5 winter, and that was by boat. Frogman Dick Hammerton is pictured navigating the road-turned-river.

Starving Children in Kingston

In Kingston, the vicious cold arrived with a vengeance after the floods had died down. On 23rd January 1895, around 10.00 am, 'a darkness settled down and simultaneously came a rushing wind from north-west by west, bearing a thick cloud of snow in large flakes and making a noise so loud as to render inaudible to many the thunder which pealed overhead in close sequence upon a flash of lightning .... almost as suddenly as the wind fell, the fall ceased, and, in a few minutes came a gleam of sunshine.'

The damage caused in Kingston by the squall was fearful. In those few brief moments, roofs had been ripped off, trees uprooted, people hurled to the ground and goods in shops and pubs ruined as the gale tore open doors and literally swept goods off shelves and counters.

By 14th February the mercury had sunk to 6F (-15C), the Surrey Comet reported. One heroine of the freeze was a Mrs Crow, landlady of the Three Compasses public house in Eden Street who cooked free hot dinners every day for children and old people. Another landlady, Mrs Jounson, who kept the Criterion public house in the Market Place, cooked sausage and mash for 100 starving children each day. An even bigger charity operation was set up at the Kingston Hotel, where Mr Petipher, the manager, made soup for 1,400 people, serving it with bread made by the Norbiton Hotel and Kingston Tannery.

Incident at Godalming

An indication of the severity of the 1895 cold spell was demonstrated in an incident at Godalming.

When the brewery of Thomas Bavistock caught fire, the water from the firemen's hoses froze so hard that when a tender from Guildford arrived it was unable to proceed up to the blaze because of the ice.

The frost was so severe in February 1895, that the Thames froze over from Richmond upwards. Here, men and children venture out on to the ice opposite the Anglers pub on the Surbiton side of Kingston town centre. When the depth of ice grew as the winter progressed, an ox was roasted at a fair held on the frozen surface of the river. The knife and fork used to carve the meat are in Kingston Museum.

Cruel Cold Winter

1895

Terrible hardships resulting from a lack of food and money made life a misery in Surrey during a long cruel winter which set in at the end of January 1895 and persisted until well into March.

Starved children flocked to soup kitchens for their only sustenance and outlying villages were isolated for weeks.

Communication with one village, Horne, near Horley, was severed for a considerable time and postmen on penny farthing bicycles were prevented from working for considerable periods.

Just before his death in 1983, Mr Cecil Johnson, a 97-year-old resident of Crowborough recalled those distressing days during the biting winter of 1894/5.

"I often feel that this cold period has never received due attention. After all, four or five generations have come and gone since that icy spell. As it occurred 85 years ago there must be very few about who can recall that icebound period. In fact it is unlikely that the present generation know anything about it or the hardships endured by their forebears.

My ninth birthday was just three months before the cold set in in January 1895. The frost and snow lasted almost unbroken until mid March 1895. Skating was continuous week after week until 28th February brought a slight thaw which made the skating surfaces wet. However, the temperatures soon fell again and skating was resumed after a few days. From the 5th February for about ten days, the mercury sunk below zero (-17C), so from 32 to over 40 degrees of frost were endured during that glacial spell.

The cold weather caused much distress and poverty amongst the working class population in my village of Horley, Surrey, then a scattered parish of

The Thames at Kingston Bridge frozen from bank to bank in February 1895. In 1814, a wooden bridge at this spot was so badly damaged by ice and frost it later had to be dismantled. The new stone bridge was constructed in 1828, and the wooden bridge was pulled down soon after.

some 3,000 persons. The inhabitants were mainly agricultural workers and smaller groups of others employed on the railway, building, brickyard and distributive trades. Farm work was impossible as the fields were covered with three to four feet of ice-capped snow for weeks. Livestock were housed in barns, cowsheds, stables and other covered buildings where they remained for weeks. Apart from feeding and the twice-daily milking of the cows, and also the cleaning of the accommodation, no other work was possible on the farms.

Generally, the main roads were kept clear but secondary roads were mostly impassable because of the frozen snow. The main London to Brighton road was kept clear and the Royal Mail coaches made the London to Brighton journey in each direction daily. The down coach changed horses at the Greyhound Hotel, Croydon; the Chequers, Horley, and, I think, near Handcross. The up coach had similar stops.

The Horley Post Office was kept by my maternal grandmother, Mrs Jane Wheeler, from 1884 until her death in 1901. During the freeze-up, postal deliveries to the outlying areas were discontinued. Before the cold set in, a postman mounted a penny farthing bicycle and took the mail to Horne daily, which was about six miles distant. All deliveries to that village were suspended until an occasional cart or trap got through and collected the accumulated mail for distribution in Horne. The mail for other outlying districts was similarly dealt with.

The effect of the cold period on the working people's households was distressing and disastrous. For them it was a very grim time. There was no work and no money in many houses for weeks. There was no unemployment benefit to fall back upon. A few loaves of bread were distributed by the Relieving Officer and sometimes a powder to make a thin soup called 'skilly' was issued.

Several ladies including my mother set up a soup kitchen in the Baptist Church School Room for children who suffered from a lack of regular meals. One day in the absence of our maid, and mother being at the soup kitchen, I had my midday meal there. It consisted of a pudding basin of good soup with a little meat and lots of vegetables. It was followed by a slice of bread from right across a large loaf, with jam on it - no butter - then a mug of cocoa. This was a very satisfying meal; the only hot dish many poor children got over the icy period.

The schools were closed during most of the cold period. The boys' school was in Horley Row and had a register of about 200. There was one slow combustion stove in the largest classroom but no heating in the other two rooms. It would have been an ice house had the school been open during those cold days.

Several boys lived three to four miles from the school, some in isolated farmhouses. For most of the hardy country boys it was a grand time when the schools closed down. Few of the pupils could have got there and most had no wish to. The girls' and infants' schools in Albert Road were also closed.

The railway was kept going and the permanent way was cleared of ice and snow at the points and other vulnerable sections. A few Horley passengers managed to travel to town daily despite the intense cold. The carriages were unheated in those days and porters carried long brass cylinders full of hot water to keep the passengers' feet warm. Many of these city men wore the customary top hat and the thickest great coat they had as they huddled together in the carriages.

I learned how to skate in a few days as did also many other boys. Learners first commenced on Lovelocks pond and when efficient, on the Brickyard pond and the lake at Langshott. They then went on to the residence of Canon Bridges. On one occasion I was skating on the moat surrounding the alleged site of Thunderfield Castle. The moat water was always noted for its clearness and I remember seeing a large carp through the ice which had been trapped by its dorsal fin. It could not have survived.

In the evenings, we skated wearing belts with bullseye lanterns attached. A bore hole made in the ice on the Brickyard pond showed the thickness to be twelve inches.

Going further afield, the Thames was frozen from Richmond upwards. Fully laden four-horse coaches crossed the river at Oxford and Wallingford. Skating took place in many London parks such as St James and Dulwich. The L.C.C. kept the ice in order and lit the lakes with flares at night. Local parties gave suppers on the banks until the late hours.

At the time, comparison was made with the great frost in the reign of Charles the second and was thought to have approached that severe period.

Altogether, it was an experience never to be forgotten by those who saw it through."

The River Wey frozen at Millmead, Guildford, yards from the town centre in 1895.

Barnes in the floods of June 1903. Today, Barnes is a busy part of the Richmond Upon Thames borough. Nearly nine inches of rain fell at Carshalton during June and at Beddington Corner near Croydon, 3.50 inches (89 mms) of rain fell in an hour on 31st May. In London, the temperature plunged in 36 hours from 83F (28C) on 1st June to 40F (5C) on 3rd, with a cold maximum of only 56F (13C) that day.

Edwardian Weather Notes

1902 A violent downpour at Surbiton gave 2 ins (50mms) in just 20 minutes on 10th September.

1903 On 30th May, George Proctor, aged 27 and Henry Charles Ebsworth aged 16 were killed by lightning while sheltering in an empty house in Croydon. Ebsworth had just remarked how beautiful the lightning was and asked if it killed people. Between 4.10 pm and 5.15 pm, 2.77 ins (71 mms) rain fell.

June went down in the records for being incredibly wet. A passage of slow moving depressions crossing southern England brought very heavy rain. At Horsley, rain fell for 60 hours non-stop from 13th. Carshalton endured a deluge on the 10th which gave 3.17 ins (80mms) and a monthly total of 8.9 ins (227mms). There then followed a three-week drought.

1906 The Great Guildford Storm occurred on 2nd August. Lives lost. Much damage.

A scorching 95F (35C) was recorded at New Malden on 1st September and at Epsom on the 2nd.

Late on Christmas night and on Boxing Day, heavy snow fell to a depth of four to six inches.

1907 On 11th April, a 'fireball' during a thunderstorm is said to have caused a blaze which severely damaged a girls school at Bramley near Godalming.

1908 An unseasonal snowfall on 24th April. The snow was clinging and wet, but gave six inches at Epsom. While most of the snow melted on the roads and paths, woodland areas were turned into Christmas card scenes. The ensuing thaw resulted in flooding in the Thames Valley.

1909 Ten inches of snow fell at Epsom on 3rd March.

The Guildford Storm

2nd August 1906

There is seldom a summer in Surrey that goes by without a thunderstorm, but fortunately few are possessed with the power and fury of the one that struck Guildford during the evening of 2nd August 1906.

The town was enjoying a heatwave and the day had been sunny but by evening the atmosphere was heavy and oppressive and soon great flashes of brilliant lightning lit up massive towering storm clouds approaching from the west.

Guildford was bathed in an eerie, lurid glow as the flashes became continuous. Then, soon after half-past eight, a fearsome squall announced the storm's arrival. The wind grew even stronger with a roar that drowned out all other sound. Chimney stacks were hurled down, trees uprooted or snapped in two and slates and tiles flung about in a terrible maelstrom of noise and destruction.

Then, suddenly all was quiet and people ventured outside to witness scenes of unimaginable chaos. Alongside Woodbridge Road several huge elms had been sent plummeting to earth, and close to The Avenue, trees had been thrown against houses smashing windows. Near this spot, in a thick tangle of branches, two people fell victim to the storm.

The lightning over Westcott.

A bedridden man escaped when the fearful storm sent a tree crashing down on his home in Shalford Road, Guildford.

A youth of 14 years and a young woman aged 23 were crushed to death whilst sheltering at the height of the furore.

At Guildford Station there was utter mayhem with masses of broken glass strewn everywhere, seats thrown onto the tracks and even heavy goods trucks derailed. Two chimney stacks toppled into the station lobby. At that very time, a Miss Steer and her brother were waiting with their bicycles for the Addlestone train. Within seconds they were showered with masonry; the bicycles were buried, but miraculously they sustained only minor injuries. Fortunately an excursion train had been delayed or several hundred children would have passed through the lobby as well.

A mighty elm tree fell against Guildford town bridge from the yard of Messrs. Moon smashing the upper part of the steel structure. Bits of zinc roofing from the cattle-market sheds in Woodbridge Road became lethal missiles, as they were propelled into the air, wrecking several shop frontages including that of Mr Ayers the baker and sub-postmaster.

In the Shalford Road district a big fir tree literally split a row of cottages in two. One of the tenants, a Mr J. Comber, aged 78, was in bed when the roof collapsed and a branch came to rest close to where he lay dazed but unhurt. The adjoining house suffered even greater destruction with plaster and masonry scattered amongst mangled furniture, the ceiling being completely torn away, but luckily the house was unoccupied at the time.

A family was made homeless in Stoughton Road when the roof was stripped completely off and the front bedroom demolished. At Loseley Park to the south-west of Guildford, the elements conspired to work their greatest mischief. Over a thousand trees were felled at all angles of the compass. At Avenue Lodge within the park, a certain Mr Sutherland, a dairyman, was blessed with particular good fortune as a lofty elm tree was hewn from the ground and sent crashing through the bedrooms. He had just discussed with his wife the fact that their children ought to have been in bed asleep but could stay up until the storm abated.

Godalming felt the full force of the storm and amongst the most bizarre of the many incidents in this location was the narrow escape of the Mousehill Brass Band whose practice session was abruptly terminated when the roof was blown off from their room adjoining the White Lion.

Intense rain fell along the path of the tempest with 1 inch (25mms) in just 17 minutes at Maori Road, Guildford and 1.46 inches (37mms) at Haslemere in 15 minutes. This is classed as a remarkable fall according to Salter in 'Rainfall of the British Isles'. Hail fell in great quantity and even eighteen hours after the storm, a double handful of cherry-sized stones was gathered at St. Catherine's.

The path of the storm took a well defined route from south-west to north-east and there was a sharp cut-off on either side; on one, scenes of turmoil and confusion; on the other, just yards away, an

Children gather firewood in the aftermath of the Guildford storm as a police officer looks on sombrely.

The site of two fatalities in the Great Storm at Guildford in August, 1906. Numerous trees block the approach to Woodbridge Avenue.

unscathed landscape. All the evidence points to the thunderstorm being accompanied by at least one tornado, a violent vortex of air around which winds can greatly exceed hurricane force.

Further damage can be caused by the much-reduced air pressure at its centre. Walls and windows can burst outwards and roofs be lifted off.

A large crowd lined the streets for the funeral the following Wednesday of the dead lad, Charles Voice, and in the address given by Sergeant Major Quittenton, the superintendent of the Salvation Army Sunday School, he remarked that 'whilst we lament in the loss of one young comrade and mourn with those who are bereaved, we cannot but think of how many have been miraculously protected, and how many open graves there might have been expected in view of the violence of the storm.'

Guildford town bridge was struck by a mighty elm.

Bramley 'Fireball'

11th April 1907

The fire-damaged shell of St Catherine's School after the storm.

Was it a fireball phenomenon - or just a brilliant lightning stroke? That was the question on many people's tongues after a school in Bramley near Godalming was set on fire in a thunderstorm on 11th April 1907.

Eye witnesses described a 'rapidly descending fireball' and postcards rushed out at the time - as was the custom during disasters in the Edwardian years - bore the caption 'The Bramley Fireball'.

In what seemed like a trifling late afternoon storm, the roof of the school was struck by lightning and blazed up at once. Fortunately, the girls of St Catherine's, built in 1886 for "gentlemen's daughters" were away for Easter holidays.

But one, who had stayed on because she was sick, was inside and had to be carried out to safety.

Guildford and Godalming Fire Brigades summoned to the scene experienced a water shortage and at the height of the blaze, huge amounts of furniture were thrown out of the school windows. Witnesses remember desks, books, pianos and curtains being carried out into the pouring rain.

Ultimately, the south west wing was rescued, but the chapel and kitchens were stripped of contents and swimming with water.

Within 48 hours of the outbreak, a nearly full meeting of the governing body under the presidency of Lord Ashcombe, was assembled on the spot.

Various alternative accommodation schemes were looked into, but with 90 girls, mistresses and servants made homeless, a major task faced the board.

Immediately after the storm, according to the Winchester Diocesan Chronicle, all the school's furniture was further spoiled by the rain that fell steadily all night and much of the next day, 'as if the skies were anxious to show that if they sent the fire they could also send the antidote to it'.

Above: *Dignified tobogganing at Epsom Downs, March 1909.* **Below:** *the Castle Grounds, Reigate, 24th April 1908.*

Derby Day Disaster

31st May 1911

A thunderstorm of amazing severity left at least five people dead and others burnt and injured just as the Epsom Derby celebrations were coming to an end in 1911.

On 31st May, the attendance at the Coronation race meeting surpassed all previous records. Despite being held a week earlier than usual because of the crowning of King George V in early June, hundreds of thousands made their way to the racecourse on a warm afternoon.

In Sutton, the High Street 'reverberated with the roar of passing traffic' heading for Epsom Downs where throngs of spectators milled on the hilly slopes of chalk and grass.

After the main race had been run, the oppressive heat of the bustling afternoon was suddenly interrupted by a few hailstones falling from an ominous-looking sky onto the roads and paths below, bouncing at angles near people's feet. Then a vivid flash of lightning, followed by a terrific clash of thunder, appeared to 'let loose all the elements and rain and hail poured down in merciless torrents'.

Parades of people leaving the races on foot and in open carriages were drenched to the skin and women dressed in summer finery 'were cruelly bedraggled'. Roads into Epsom turned into muddy rivers and the soaked human army came to a near standstill.

A party of 20 took shelter against the wall of the reservoir on Banstead Downs, and eight of them were struck by lightning. Two men were killed on the spot and were removed to Banstead Mortuary, while the injured were taken to Sutton Hospital by ambulance and motor car.

Among the injured were two young men from Plaistow, London, and a middle aged man from Ilford. A policeman on point duty was also transported to hospital. George Curran, aged 25, and William Storr, aged 21, from West Ham and Lower Sydenham, were both killed. A bicycle nearby had its handlebars broken by the lightning, and Curran's boots were split.

Also hit was a Sutton postman, William Teddar, from Haddon Road, who sustained severe injuries to his left side. He was cycling from the Downs, and on reaching the reservoir, which is near Belmont Station, remarked to a colleague, "I think I'll get off and get shelter under this wall." Hardly had he dismounted when he was struck and knocked unconscious. A police constable Pain, from Dulwich, who was also struck was barely able to move but managed to ask the occupants of a passing cart to "procure assistance." One of the victims was conveyed to hospital by a coster named Short and travelling in the same carriage was his son, Nipper Short, the juvenile pearly king dressed in full paraphernalia of office.

Another man, George Arthur, from Westminster, was also knocked down by lightning at Worcester Park.

In commenting on the tragedy at Banstead Downs, the coroner said at the inquest that it was probable that a wet bowler hat, worn by one of the deceased, would have attracted the lightning. Burn marks were found on Storr's back and under an armpit.

Back at the racecourse, among the unfortunate victims of the afternoon's violent storm was a young greengrocer called Wilfrid Noah Wetherall, who was aged just 17, and who worked at Beddington near Croydon.

His terrible fate at Buckle's Gap went unnoticed for some time as the thunder crashed above and the lightning flashed all around. His employer's horse became very frightened and would not stop jerking its head. Several people tried to restrain the terrified animal and called for young Wilfrid to help. It was then that he was seen sitting in the back of the cart with his hand raised as if to ward off a blow. It was assumed he had been hit by the same flash which had disturbed the horse.

A remarkable fact was that the crown of the straw hat he was wearing had been cut out by the lightning, and the brim had slipped over his face. News of his death came as a great shock to those all around, some of whom had been 'rendered quite deaf for a considerable time'.

At the Epsom mortuary, the lad was found to have a fern-leaf design on his body and it was presumed that he had been struck by the same lightning which led to the horse's death. At the boy's inquest, a survivor said he had seen a ball of fire and that he had tasted sulphuric acid in his mouth.

In a tent at Tattenham Corner, tragedy was narrowly avoided when eight men from Peckham, working as jobmasters, were struck. One, a man aged 50, sustained serious injury. He suffered extensive shock to the system, loss of muscle action in the right arm, and burns on the right arm and left leg. A policeman was also hit at Buckle's Gap.

As if the grim toll wasn't enough, another man from Sutton by the name of James Harris of Benhill Road, was leaning on some rails near the racecourse when they were struck. He was unconscious for two hours and was taken to Epsom Cottage Hospital.

The mayhem was not restricted to the Downs. A young City policeman while riding his bicycle in London Road, Morden was caught in the storm, and subsequently his dead body was found near Garth Road. Girls from the City of London Imperial Cadet Yeomanry gave artificial respiration but he died of cardiac paralysis.

The family of Mr Alfred Mizen of Lonesome Road, Mitcham, had an 'affrightening experience' when the lightning struck the roof of his house, tore the plaster off the walls and filled the rooms with dust, and in Church Road, a line post was struck and 'shivered into a heap of shavings'. Wimbledon Fire Station's roof was set on fire.

For those scared of thunderstorms, there could not have been a worse time. Miss Anne Overall, aged 65, of Kingston Road, Merton, became dreadfully frightened owing to the heavy peals of thunder. She went to a neighbour's house at about 4 o'clock and told them that the thunder and lightning was making her terribly frightened. She was taken back to her residence a little later, and after again saying she was frightened by the storm, 'gave a heavy sigh and fell dead'.

Enormous amounts of rain fell during that wicked Wednesday afternoon. At White Hill, Caterham, 2.97 ins (75mms) was recorded, and at Burgh Heath, Banstead, 1.75 ins (43mms) was measured. But the greatest downpour was logged at Banstead Hall, where 3.59 ins (92mms) cascaded down.

At Bletchingley, 1.94ins (48mms) of rain fell between 5pm and 7pm. Three houses were struck by lightning and a wall and motor house wrecked. One woman was hurt and three children were slightly injured.

'Never within the memory of any living person has such a storm been experienced as that which broke over Bletchingley at about six o'clock on Wednesday evening,' the Dorking and Leatherhead Advertiser reported.

Immense quantities of bricks, concrete and mortar were strewn over Bletchingley village when a motor garage and the walls bordering Castle Cottage were struck. Down the road, the wife of Mr Edward Daniels was hit by a powerful stroke which punched three large holes in the ceiling of a bedroom. She sustained burns to the arms and legs, and her clothing was scorched.

Cowering in the house next door was an eight-year old girl, Dora Huggett. While her guardians went to fetch help for Mrs Daniels, another vicious flash struck, and damaged the petrified girl's home, leaving zig-zag fractures in the walls. She, too, had been hit, but fortunately survived the ordeal. 'She was quite black in the face and foamed at the mouth', said the newspaper, adding that 'much crockery in the house was smashed'. In another neighbour's cottage, lightning pierced through bedroom ceilings and Charles Hatfield, aged 10, was hit and sustained a long scar on his chest, exactly like the leaf of a fern. Villagers arrived with brandy for the injured, and they all eventually recovered.

At Merstham, trains were halted when 60 tons of chalk and mud collapsed onto the tracks at Hooley. A train from Charing Cross carrying theatre-goers did not reach Redhill until almost 2am - seven hours after leaving London.

In Bletchingley's Brewer Street, water was three feet in the road and at Godstone, hail the size of marbles lay six inches deep on the Bletchingley Road and horses had to rescue motor cars unable to negotiate the huge piles of ice. In Tadworth, too, the hail was so fierce that pedestrians and cyclists' hands were left bleeding, and at the North Looe smallholdings in Ewell, 50 chickens were drowned.

At an inquest into the Derby deaths the coroner informed the jury that he had heard many people say the storm was a judgement on those who visited the races, and he stigmatised the remark as 'a very foolish one'.

The inquest also studied the bizarre fact that when the lightning killed young Wetherall and the horse, those sitting between them in the van were incredibly not affected.

The trail of destruction at Castle Cottage, Bletchingley after the thunderstorm on Derby Day 1911

Unrest on the Weather Front

1911 Ferocious thunderstorm over Surrey on 31st May killing several race-goers after the Derby. A hot summer followed with some exceptional temperatures. Mr S. G. Russell at Parkside, Ashley Road, Epsom, logged 98F (36.7C) in his official screen on 9th August.

1914 Another killer thunderstorm in Mitcham and environs on 14th June, ten days after Britain declared war on Germany.

1916 A chilling end to February with some deep snow which the troops helped to clear. At Walton on the Hill, 21 ins of snow fell between 23rd and 28th February.

1917 Frost in February penetrated the soil to a depth of 9 ins. Snow lay to a depth of 5 ins at Byfleet. The first part of April was very cold and snowy. In early spring, bushes at Nutfield were burnt by the icy winds.

1918 Very destructive hailstorm with stones up to 2½ ins in length on 16th July.

1919 During the night of 27th April, a moist sticky snowstorm attained a depth of 10 ins at Purley.

1921 Pirbright Pond dried up for the first time in years during a prolonged drought. Frimley and Weybridge had less than 11ins (275mms) of rain in the year - only half the usual amount. It was the driest year known.

1923 Phenomenal electrical storm with thousands of flashes an hour on the night of 9th July.

1927 The Great Boxing Day Blizzard. One of the worst snowstorms this century.

1928 Melting snow led to much flooding in January.

1929 A particularly cold February with some severe frosts. On 13th, it was 10F (-12C) at Redhill.

Troops clear deep snow from Lesbourne Road, Reigate, in February 1916. They are pictured outside the Lesbourne Halls, now re-named the Desert Rat. The little chap with the hat on the right is Eric Neill whose father was the publican.

Crowds gather to witness the flooding in Mitcham.

Blood-Red Tempest South London

14th June 1914

By John Bradbury

The morning of Sunday, 14th June 1914, was not noticeably so very different from any other, being such as you would hope for in early summer. The sun, unchecked by cloud, shone continuously as little children on Wandsworth Common played bat and ball, tag, or 'ring-a-roses' in the shade of tall elm trees. A lazy dog, sprawling in freshly mowed grass, blinked and yawned as he reviewed a flotilla of mallard ducks swimming to and fro in their perennial quest for food.

In that breathless heat a solitary model yacht, becalmed and abandoned by her phantom crew, lay tantalisingly out of reach of a tearful child standing forlorn and helpless by the water's edge.

The last days of innocence, basking peacefully in the Edwardian aftermath, were slipping silently away, like the unseen sands of time. Soon all this, and much more, would be engulfed by a cataclysmic struggle.

But for the time being all was well. Church bells chimed as the starched and sturdy middle class,

Transport to Purley and South Croydon was hampered by the deep floods at Norbury after the terrible thunderstorm of 14th June 1914.

attired in their sensible Sunday best, crocodiled into the parish churches, giving just a few thoughts to the impending war.

Along the tidy suburban streets off Wandsworth Common, a hundred Sunday joints were already sizzling in copious ovens, when the sun, turned suddenly sullen in an increasingly liverish sky. But nobody took any notice, even though volleys of still-distant thunder heralded impending tragedy.

The giant storm that broke over South London was a phenomenon quite outside the previous experience of any who lived through it. At high noon, day became night - illuminated by sheets of blood red lightning and accompanied by a racketting thunder seemingly orchestrated by a malevolent intent on an evil outcome to the excesses of Nature's power.

The rain splashed onto parched pavements before descending in a watery mass, soon followed by a barrage of hailstones, some as big as walnuts. 'Windows were smashed', reported the News Chronicle, 'bringing with it a trail of terror and havoc to the neighbourhood.'

'A man with clothes afire ran screaming along Windmill Road in the direction of the Patriotic Asylum. Struck by lightning, he was badly burnt about the midriff and the gold watch and chain he wore had turned black.'

'Beneath a planetree, in a hollow called 'Frying Pan', five terrified children tried to shelter from the storm; their tiny faces buried against the bark of the tree. An eye witness standing at some distance, later said, "Hell visited Wandsworth Common this afternoon", and went on, "a ball of crimson fire enveloped the tree, simultaneous thunder shook the very ground on which we stood". Three of the five children fell to the ground. The two survivors staggered away to collapse into a roadside ditch. The fallen children were beyond medical help - they must have died instantly, for their mouths gaped, their eyes bulged and their faces were as black as burnt toast.'

At the very height of the storm an old man, long since unaccustomed to great physical exertion, was observed running along Bolingbroke Grove gesticulating with a walking cane. When others dashed from shelter to halt his headlong rush, he used the stick to beat off those who would delay him. A few yards further on his fragile frame crumpled by the kerbside, and only fear-filled eyes, more eloquent than the spoken word told of a terror bridled only by panic. He died three days later.

On the other side of the common, several families stood beneath an old oak tree, well known as a 'trysting place', surrounded by a wooden seat. Following a lull, the storm once more gathered strength and struck with terrible ferocity, this time swallowing the oak tree in a sea of flame and claiming four more lives. The dead included Marion Grist, of Lindore Road, Battersea. Her fiance, Percy West, lay beside her terribly injured. Albert Button, aged 21, of Chivalry Road, Wandsworth, died with his three year old daughter Florence, who had hid her head in fear beneath her father's raincoat. As for Mrs Munday, of Steelworks Road, Battersea, she died at Bolingbroke Hospital. But miraculously, her baby escaped uninjured.

Not within living memory had a thunderstorm in this country caused such loss of life, injury and general havoc. In 45 minutes more than two inches of rain fell, flooding many basement flats from Clapham Junction to Fernlea Road, Balham. Under the heading 'Comedy At Balham', the Wandsworth Boro' News described how a family in Fernlea Road were about to have their Sunday dinner when the father noticed that, 'The iron covering of the manhole in their basement flat was being lifted by the pressure of water. Like a man of resource, he stood on the cover and called on his son to add his weight, but, continued the report, 'Man is a puny animal in the hands of nature and within a minute both men found themselves thrown aside as water poured into the flat. Before long there was 5ft of water in the dining room and the table carrying their meal of roast beef and Yorkshire pudding was last seen floating upstairs towards the front door'.

In the area of Wandsworth Common eleven people were struck by lightning. Seven of them died. Undoubtedly a storm of tropical intensity, the News Chronicle, of Monday 15th June, carried the headline, 'Wandsworth's Red Sunday', a reference to the lightning variously described as blood-red, crimson, or violet. The thunder, in itself harmless, was such that it terrified even those who would not normally react.

While the storm raged south of the river, families in northern suburbs continued to bask in the sun, pausing only to flick away a particularly troublesome blow fly. The following morning they were surprised to discover that, for once, their southern cousins had captured the worst of the weather.

Records kept by a Dorking meteorologist at the time show that Sunday, 14th June, 1914 was a day with a maximum of 75F (24C) and a humidity of 79 per cent. No rain fell at Dorking, such was the local nature of the storm.

A Terrible Hailstorm

16th July 1918

The incidence of damaging hail in the UK is greatest in the South East with Surrey and South London suffering the most, according to research by Perry.

A good example was the Great East Surrey Hailstorm which cut a characteristic swathe of destruction from near Dorking, east of Kingswood through Coulsdon, and Kenley to Addington in the early hours of 16th July 1918.

An eye witness account described how at Buckland, west of Reigate, terrific thunder and lightning preceded the climax. A loud roaring noise was heard and dense hail obscured the light. Greenhouses were riddled, window panes smashed, trees stripped and vegetables of all kinds pulverised.

The destruction was confined to a strip 800 yards wide inside which everything growing had been laid waste, whereas adjoining land remained unscathed.

The most severe phase of the storm took place between Coulsdon and Kenley. Hailstones here were two and a half inches in length and some attained the size of pigeon eggs, whilst others had protuberances and spikes nearly an inch long. Glass and crops alone at Canehill near Chipstead suffered an estimated £1,000 of damage. Three cubic yards of hail was collected from the gutters the following morning by the hospital groundsmen.

In the Riddlesdown area fields of grain were beaten down and cut to pieces. Cabbages were reduced to pulp and at Briton Hill Road masses of hail cascading off a roof buried rose bushes to a depth of two feet. Paint work was scored and soot-covered stones rolled down chimneys and bounded across rooms knocking against walls and furniture.

Torrential rain fell as well, and caused thousands of tons of soil, pebbles and rocks to be washed down the steep slopes on the north west side of Croham Hurst.

A similar though much less severe example took place in the very thundery June of 1980. On the 24th at 12.30 pm an intense fall stripped plants of flowers and leaves and piles of hail still littered gardens in the late evening. The track of this storm followed the same path as its predecessor, and drivers were forced to abandon their cars and seek shelter in shops alongside the A22 road at Kenley near Purley.

Nightmare for Brontophobics

A strong contender for the title 'storm of the century' must include the one that spectacularly took place on the night of 9th July 1923. The brilliance and frequency of the lightning strokes, the loudness of its thunder and the fact that it went on all night with unremitting torrential rain made it a formidable storm. For brontophobics - those with a fear of thunder - it was a nightmare come true.

The storm was really a series of thunderstorm cells which tracked north from France and then cut a swathe across Sussex, Surrey and London before petering out in Lincolnshire.

An observer at Claygate described the lightning as being a beautiful violet colour. The whole southern horizon was ablaze, but at first there was only an occasional low rumble of thunder and not a breath of wind to ease the sweltering conditions.

The storm struck in earnest during the late evening - at Croydon around 10 pm - and raged for nearly eight hours. Thunder blasted like the firing of field guns, a sound still fresh in the minds of those who had not long returned from the Western Front. Children awoke panic stricken. Many buildings were struck. Rain cascaded like a celestial waterfall. On occasion there would be a brief lull before the pyrotechnics returned with renewed vigour.

At Walton on the Hill an eye-witness said a ball of fire dropped in front of a house and within minutes it was completely engulfed in flames.

Mr Spencer Russell using a brontometer, an instrument enabling him to measure the number of lightning flashes counted nearly 7,000 with a peak intensity of 47 per minute between 11 pm and midnight. Four hours later at his Chelsea observatory there were still up to 37 per minute.

Lightning damaged houses in Wallington, Carshalton, Mitcham and Headley and at Nutfield, fields of corn were laid flat by the sheer force of the rain.

At New Malden, 2.91 inches (74mm) or some 11 per cent of the annual rainfall was measured. At Banstead there was 2.8 inches, Lowfield Heath 2.75 inches but at Wormley and Godalming very little rain fell.

Several thunderstorms occurred in Surrey during the hot summer of 1983. This storm, at Tandridge, near Oxted, struck an old tree in Tandridge Churchyard.

The Tatsfield and Biggin Hill area was marooned for four days after the heavy snows on Boxing Day 1927. Villagers were asked to lay out black clothes on the snow so aeroplanes could drop food parcels. Eventually a passage two feet wide was cut through the ice to re-establish contact with the outside world.

South Godstone veterinary surgeon Mr Glover (in the bowler hat) found a sensible way to travel to Godstone Green after the 1927 snowstorm.

Boxing Day Blizzard

December 1927

Christmas Day 1927 dawned dull and gloomy and for most of the day relentless heavy rain lashed down as families indoors tried to prevent the atrocious weather from dampening their festive spirits.

In the murk outside, muddy puddles grew larger by the hour as the downpour continued and roads were awash after days of unceasing rain. At Redhill there had been nearly two and a half inches (68mms) since 20th December, and it seemed inevitable that serious flooding would take place.

What followed took most people by surprise, for as the light faded and a slight chill lowered the 46F (8C) recorded earlier in the day, the raindrops turned increasingly to sleet... and then large white flakes.

By late evening, as relatives set out for their homeward journeys, carrying bags full of Christmas presents, a fully fledged snowstorm blew up. Even Surrey's well-off families driving brand new, four-cylinder Humbers, costing £250, would have found the going tough as the century's worst blizzard began to bare its teeth on that wild Christmas night.

By midnight, savage winds whipped over the North Downs at Banstead, Reigate and Caterham, driving the snow into deep drifts. On Boxing Day morning, Surrey awoke to an incredible white winter wonderland - with scenes more realistic than those on traditional Christmas cards.

Icy blasts of wind whistled through north-facing windows as horizontal snow brought white-out conditions across the county, piling the flakes into drifts up to 20 feet on roads over the Surrey hills.

Residents in and around Tatsfield ventured out to find snow piled up to 15 feet deep.

The main road at Reigate Hill was buried under snow nearly ten feet deep.

Boxing Day had a maximum temperature of just 32F (0C), and in the strong northerly wind, anyone not suitably dressed would have been in great danger from frostbite or exposure.

The following day, Tuesday 27th December, unveiled a county gripped by the worst Arctic conditions known by its residents. Villages such as Chaldon, Tatsfield, Farleigh and Chelsham near Croydon, were marooned for almost a week. Little children who ventured out at Tilburstow Hill, South Godstone, were photographed under 15 feet snow drifts, which towered above them, snarling menacingly. At Reigate Hill, crowds of sightseers scaled cumbersome drifts to reach the windswept summit near the top of Gatton Bottom, where they were able to walk over the tops of signposts and have their pictures taken by friends. At Effingham, a bus had to be dug out of a 14 feet drift, and in Kingston, a man and a boy skied into the deserted marketplace while a snowplough cleared the road between the town and Winter's Bridge, Long Ditton.

On Wednesday 28th December, a north easterly gale blasted the snow into greater drifts which attained a strange beauty in the dazzling sunshine.

By Saturday 31st December, fears were growing for villages cut off by the mountainous heaps of snow and the Salvation Army chartered five aeroplanes to drop food supplies to isolated communities. The previous day, a D. H. 60 plane, piloted by Captain Hope, set off from Stag Lane aerodrome and circled over Surrey, but due to poor light was unable to release its packets of groceries, and on that day, Croydon was listed as the coldest place in Britain with 21 degrees of frost (-12C) at dawn. The BBC asked people to lay out black clothes in the snow 'not less than 15 feet in diameter' to help the pilots pinpoint people in need across an area between Redhill, Lingfield, Addington and Sevenoaks.

The front page of the Daily Express on 31st December carried remarkable stories of the great blizzard. 'Glacier Near London - 8ft Waves Of Ice On A Main Road' was how the Croydon to Warlingham route was described.

'The main road from Croydon to Warlingham, by way of Sanderstead, which in the ordinary way is a busy omnibus route, is completely blocked by frozen snowdrifts for a considerable distance. It is impossible to traverse it even on foot.'

Vividly describing the scene, the broadsheet newspaper continued: 'Mr A. H. Jannaway, owner of the Cherry Tree Fruit and Poultry Farm, Sanderstead, telephoned to the Daily Express office

Two schoolboys are dwarfed by 15 feet drifts at Tilburstow Hill, Godstone, in December 1927.

last night:- "We have been cut off from the outer world since Monday night. The road from Sanderstead village to my poultry farm - a distance of about half a mile - presents the appearance of a glacier; the great waves of snow varying in height from four to eight feet. It is impossible to use the road, and Croydon can only be reached by making a detour on foot across ploughed fields and over hedges.

"The snow is even deeper where the main road continues from Hamsey Green to Warlingham. Efforts are being made at Warlingham to cut a track through in our direction but the snow there is nine feet deep.

"My farm, with the little cluster of nine cottages around it, is completely isolated as regards supplies of food by road. We made up a sledge party yesterday in order to get bread and meat, only to find that at Warlingham, the bread was sold out.

"On our way we passed two other sledges, one bearing a milk churn and the other carrying an injured girl. It took us two hours to cover the mile journey. We also passed the tops of two carts which were completely snowed in.

"It was no easy task to get our sledge home, for not only was the surface of the snow uneven, but in places the crust of the snow was treacherous and we sank almost to our waists.

"We had hard work on the farm digging out the dogs in their kennels and clearing the snow from the chicken houses.'"

Stories like this are remembered by a number of elderly residents in the district. Mrs Doris Cook of Bletchingley remembered 60 years on how, as a young woman working as a maid at a large house in Merstham, she was terrified that her employers may not accept the snow as a reason for not getting to work. Her father carried her two miles through perilous conditions so she could prove loyalty.

In Guildford, streets were buried under a foot of snow and the Hogs Back was completely blocked. Three buses and a lorry were buried within two miles of Guildford town centre.

High up on Box Hill, hundreds enjoyed the sudden

ski resort facilities. Some, it is said, dazzled the natives with splashes of orange, green, red and black in their costumes, built on the bathing pattern, with little wicked caps, and a dash of crimson round the tops of their socks. But the rain down at Merstham, caused a landslide on the railway line which stopped trains.

By New Year's Eve, many main roads such as the London to Brighton route were passable with care, although many hilly thoroughfares had become narrow passages between walls of snow up to 10 feet high, and the Bagshot to Basingstoke road, west of Hook, Hants, was still blocked.

On 1st January 1928, a slight rise in temperature to 38F (3.5C) at Redhill, turned the deep snow to slush in low-lying parts of Surrey and posed a threat to the popular skating activities. Sites were plentiful with two square miles of frozen floodwater at and around The Hollows at Chertsey; near-perfect ice rink conditions at Staines Rugby Club, and conditions so good at Weston Green Football Club, Thames Ditton, that an ice yacht was seen 'sailing effectively'.

On 2nd January, the young Mr Christopher Bull, a keen weather observer at Redhill, recorded .92ins (23mms) of rain as the mercury in the thermometer rose a little more. This caused disastrous flooding in the vicinity of the River Thames.

The Surrey Comet reported on New Year's Eve how, 'Already the Thames and its many tributaries have got far beyond themselves, and tremendous lakes, in some places a couple of miles across, are to be seen throughout the middles reaches. In the low-lying parts everywhere, flood water stretches across the meads, in some cases covered by a thin film of ice. Bungalows are isolated, and many roads are impassable through flood or because their surface is ice-sheeted'.

Melting snow caused floods at the factory gate in Ruskin Avenue, Richmond on 7th January 1928.

Thames Ditton bore the brunt of some of the invading waters and the local council provided a horse and cart which, 'plies to and fro for the benefit of the local residents near the level crossing'. But beyond the railway, the fields were so awash that the carts were, 'axle-deep and the horses could scarcely keep their feet'.

When the flood was at its very height and the guardian of the Styx had brought a cargo safely through the river, a woman came splashing through the turmoil in thigh boots. The swirling waters lapped above her knees and she besought the driver to come along uncharted ways to her aid, for she had a sick husband and her son, 'must go for the doctor and he has no boots for this weather'. The driver doubted his ability to make the passage, 'but his suppliant brought courage with her', convincing him she knew every inch of the way.

'At the Swan ferry, Thames Ditton, the huts which usually house the tackle of punt and skiff, the beer jars which serve as water carriers in summer and the cushions and paddles of finer days, were almost adrift on the swell of the waters. Several houseboats sunk nearby. The Cosy Nook broke adrift at Hampton Court and was carried into mid stream with only its flagmast showing. When last seen, the furnished boat was being swept away into the darkness at Thames Ditton.'

Residents of Giggs Hill, near Long Ditton complained to the police of boys and youths indulging in snowballing battles in the vicinity of houses and to the dangers to passers-by.

The Surrey Comet reported, 'During the course of one snowballing episode, the plate glass window of Mr G. Page's shop at Winter's Bridge was broken by a misdirected snowball'.

At East Molesey, the beautiful cricket ground, lined with deckchairs beneath tall elms in summer, was completely submerged, and ice yachting took place.

One family set out in a boat, from Sunbury Court Island and braving the torrents, returned to the island with a turkey and two chickens. A policeman, meanwhile, rescued a woman from the icy waters at Markway Bridge, Sunbury, by diving in and struggling for 20 minutes to bring her to the banks.

By 2nd January, the continuing thaw swelled the waters even further, and on the 3rd, 25 laden craft

Carrying out the spade work after the 1927 snowstorm. The picture is believed to have been taken at Bletchingley.

were adrift with seven sunk in the Thames above Kingston Bridge. Each carried a hundred tons of Swedish planks and were moored for loading when they were unleashed by the raging torrents.

'Once they were caught in the vortex, the barges were carried at great speed towards Kingston Bridge, where they struck the buttresses with a resounding crash that made the solid stone structure seem to shiver from end to end.'

The Surrey Comet noted how the strident tones of the sirens of the tug which went to rescue the barges, 'caused considerable excitement in the vicinity of Kingston Bridge, which was quickly crowded with people who witnessed a spectacle rarely seen on the Thames'.

It observed that a posse of police, fearing that the bridge may have been damaged by the blow, removed the throngs of people. Some of the craft broke free again from under the arches and collided with a flotilla of timber barges at the Grindley, Miskin and Company's wharf. Two of these were sunk. Five barges continued on their escapade to freedom, and carried with them three pleasure launches. The boats shot off to Teddington Lock where one of the barges crashed into the posts of the weir and became jammed, and another capsized in the lock. Volunteers up and down the Thames joined forces to try and seize the wreckage from the barges in the shape of loose planks which became wedged under the bridge arches.

At Hinchley Wood, Manor Road was flooded to a depth not known in most people's lifetime and the services of the Esher and Dittons motor fire engine were required. In Thames Ditton, Station Road was flooded along the whole length and planks were set up for people to use the station.

The Esher to Hersham road was not passable and on one occasion, buses to Chertsey and Staines had to be diverted via Cobham and Seven Hills. The village of West End, Esher, was badly hit by flooding, as was the Hare Lane Green at Claygate. London General Omnibuses became lost at Long Arch, Thames Ditton.

On 4th January, the seething waters of the Thames brought more drama and bungalow owners on Sunbury Court Island had to chase furniture in their gardens, whilst families were rescued from the Creek estate through the windows of their homes.

In Molesey, police waded around in bare feet, carrying their socks and shoes and the ambulance station was unreachable due to deep water. The Karsino was so inundated that water halved the island and flowed beneath the bandstand from one

Motor vehicles were buried completely on the North Downs near Reigate and Redhill.

side of the river to the other, and Palm Beach was invisible. A bride was carried by her chauffeur over floodwaters after her wedding at Shepperton Church and in the Harry Offer boathouse an otter was discovered next to a headless fish it had apparently fed off. At Watersplash Road, Shepperton, a woman waded out to rescue a parrot from her marooned home. 'Gum-booted she gingerly picked her way through the floods and on her return to terra firma, carrying the cage high above her, she was cheered by the onlookers.'

In Walton Road, Molesey, a butcher carried on with his business, carving his joints, although the top of his counter was only just visible above the floodwaters. Other traders chased tins round their shops in an endeavour to find what customers wanted.

Reports suggested that many Molesey homes were flooded and that the girls school at East Molesey was open all night on Wednesday, 4th January, to accommodate families who had to leave their dwellings. It was also chronicled that, 'in West Molesey, hundreds of poor people were affected'.

As if to rub salt in the wound, the blizzard and floods were followed by a gale. Floodwaters in the Kingston area were said to have been whipped up to give the appearance of a 'storm-tossed sea in miniature'.

At Hampton Court, traffic was dislocated when a branch, one foot across, was torn from a tree and fell onto overhead tramway lines, and at Kempton Park, a train ran over the roof of a chicken house. Major L. A. L. Carter escaped death when a huge tree trunk fell on his motor, injuring him, and at Thames Ditton, a large hole was punched in the church roof when a chimney shaft toppled.

The rest of January 1928 continued very wet but as if to make amends for the Arctic conditions Mother Nature provided generally mild weather for the remainder of the month.

Awesome floods at Mill Mead, Guildford on 3rd January 1928 as the snow melted.

Sixty years on – in 1987 – towering snowdrifts at Titsey Hill almost equalled those of 1927.

Sightseers traverse the mountainous snowdrifts on Reigate Hill in 1927.

After the snow came the floods. Woking and many other Surrey towns were swamped.

Floods damaged shops in Guildford in January 1928. This was the watery scene at Cauldron's, the drapers, in the High Street at the junction with Friary Street.

Flooding in Marketfield Road, Redhill, 1935.

A Glance at the Thirties

Homes in Marketfield Road, Redhill (above), were badly damaged in a flash flood on 25th June 1935. The downpour lasted just over an hour and was set off by storm clouds which built up after a heatwave. In Dorking the temperature is reported to have dropped from 85F to 68F (29 to 20C) in just a short while. Torrential rain broke out accompanied by hail stones 'the size of cherries'. Inside 15 minutes, the centre of Dorking was completely under water, with a flood of muddy rainwater cascading down Dene Street into the High Street and then on into Ansell Road and Rothes Road. Stones and debris were washed down from Chequers Yard into the High Street and Pump Corner 'resembled Brighton beach'. Assistants in Woolworth's store, paddled ankle deep and the Fire Brigade pumped out flooded cellars at Down, Scott and Down. In Redhill, the temperature exceeded 80F (27C) on 12 days during the summer, following a cold May.

1930 A severe gale felled many trees on 12th January. Phone lines down. 77 mph gusts at Croydon Airport.

1931 A cool summer with nothing above 76F (25C) at Redhill.

1933 The driest year of all in East Surrey between 1926 and 1979. 87F (31C) was recorded at Merstham on 27th July and 6th August.

1938 On 25th January, weather watcher Mr Christopher Bull noted that the aurora, or northern lights, were clearly visible from Redhill. Red streaks and flashes were seen in the sky. Part of Redhill town was under 18 inches of water after a storm on 12th August which struck an ice cream seller from Reigate. Christmas was a 'white' one, after a cold spell set in on 17th December. The snow lay seven inches deep in Redhill by Boxing Day, but thereafter melted

1939 A short cold snap at the end of December sent temperatures plummeting to 12F (-11C) on 29th.

A real Christmas card scene at the Lakers Hotel, Redhill, in December 1938. Snow started to fall on 19th December and by Boxing Day, 7½ inches lay. All floodlighting had to cease when wartime blackouts were ordered the following year.

An Icy War-time Winter

January 1940

No weather forecasts were issued during the war years for fear that the information may have been used to disadvantage by the enemy, so it came as a shock to the people of Surrey when some of the harshest weather this century arrived in January 1940.

The Surrey Comet summed up the restrictions as 'one of the greatest misfortunes for which Hitler has so far been responsible'.

After a cold foggy Christmas in 1939, the bitter weather soon moved in and with no street lights being illuminated, there were many road accidents in the darkness. In thick fog at Wimbledon, spectators at a football match remarked how it was only by sound they could guess what the score was. When the fog cleared by 27th December, heavy snow fell and a girl died when she slipped in front of a van at Sunbury. A brief thaw in early January gave way to vicious easterly winds, sending the temperature down to 18F (-8C) at Kingston. The powdery snow blew through Kingston Market Place as housewives tried to shop around for food to overcome the meat rations and shortages of butter and sugar.

The Thames froze over at Kingston and ice-breakers tried to keep a channel open for boats. On the trolley buses there were great problems.

Big Freeze, 1947

Council workmen shovel snow from Redhill High Street in the 1947 winter.

Times were still hard following the second world war. Foodstuffs were not always plentiful and a shortage of coal sometimes meant families huddling around empty grates.

So when the winds swung to the east in the third week of January, bringing a prolonged period of snow, ice and leaden skies until the middle of March, it seemed that nature had dealt a cruel blow.

Heavy snow fell on the night of 23rd January threatening a concert at the Epsom Institution put on by Sutton's Sea Rangers for the district's old folk. Mr John Wright, who trained the cadets choir, was stuck in his car at the height of the blizzard and failed to attend.

Next day, on the snow-covered airfield at Croydon Airport, a terrible disaster occurred when 12 people lost their lives within a few minutes of bidding farewell to relatives and friends on the edge of the icy field. The Dakota airliner in which they were travelling was bound for South Africa, but moments after take off, it faltered, dipped and crashed onto a stationary, smaller Dakota plane. In a flash, both craft went up in flames. Among those who perished were a family of four from Queens Road, Weybridge. Mr and Mrs T. H. G. Cond, their son, aged 2½, and baby of five months, all died. They were setting off to start a new life abroad.

One passenger, Mr F. J. Ridsdale, a solicitor, of Westlands, West Byfleet, managed to claw his way

The winters of 1940 and 1947 are famous for their cold spells. This picture shows the frozen Thames at East Molesey on 24th January 1940.

out, and another dramatic escape was made by Mr and Mrs Ingram of Hartley Old Road, Purley, who jumped to safety, Mrs Ingram doing so while her hair was ablaze.

In the early days of the big freeze, the icy weather was the talk of the town. Those who ventured out made sure they were equipped for the Arctic conditions. In the unheated Banstead Institute Hall, shivering crowds gathered to watch a play, 'Hawk Island', put on by the Good Companions. The Banstead Herald said it was a 'thriller with some spine-chilling moments that only added to the atmosphere of a refrigeration plant!'.

'Making their way to the Institute over snow-covered roads the audiences found themselves faced with the bleak prospect of sitting for over two hours in acute discomfort. Wise people who were prepared to sink their pride brought hot water bottles and cuddled them throughout the evening, and others wrapped themselves in rugs and managed to take an intelligent interest in the proceedings.'

Animals were cold, too. Wood fires were lit in the cages at Chessington Zoo and there was concern about a lioness, named Sally, who was expecting offspring.

In Sutton, the power cuts hit hard. By the end of February, 1,500 extra people were unemployed, due to blackouts and 400 were temporarily laid off because of the frosts which hit the building trade.

Long queues for coal developed and at Sutton High Street, many people arrived at the Wandsworth and District Gas Company's works, in search of solid fuel to keep their homes warm in the severe weather. The Sutton Herald commented on 14th February, 'Practically every day during the cold spell there has been a queue at the works of persons anxious to obtain coke. This they have carried away in barrows, perambulators and all kinds of odd containers'. The Sutton and Cheam area suffered power cuts of up to six hours at a time, and the council's municipal offices had neither heat nor lights for a week in mid-February. Staff worked in overcoats to the light of candles and hurricane lamps, but in Surrey factories failing to be classed as performing essential work, power was completely cut off.

One resident, Mr Charles Hartwell of Malden Road, Cheam, came up with a tip for housewives struggling to manage in the power cuts. He suggested using up-turned biscuit tins for cooking food by firesides. Potatoes, and vegetarian nut rissoles could be baked inside them, he claimed.

As the bitter weather continued unabated, people's tempers grew short. One man from Ridge Road, Sutton, appeared in court after a snowball hit him in the face while he was inside his car, causing him to skid. He grabbed two boys and rubbed their faces in the snow, but was later charged with assault. He pleaded 'guilty under great provocation'.

On the morning of 24th February, Mr Christopher Bull recorded his lowest temperature of the century

Lying six hundred feet up on the North Downs, the villages of Tatsfield, Biggin Hill and Cudham suffered from the deepest snow in 1947. Here, the 471 bus and a milk van are being rescued from the drifts at Cudham Lane.

when the mercury plunged to just 1F (-17C) at Gatton Point, Redhill, after a still starry night, with the snow-covered ground glistening in the hard frost. When the sun shone that morning, it 'burned' Mr Bull's neck. He had almost forgotten what sunshine was after three weeks of endless dull wintry weather.

At Beddington, near Croydon, housewives did not need to be reminded how cold it was at the end of February. When they asked why some butchers were not getting their fair share of offal, deputy mayor Alderman J. Vale asked questions at the Beddington and Wallington food control committee meeting at the Town Hall, Wallington. He was told that sacks of frozen tails could not be separated even with a chopper, and that ox livers were welded together inside the bags.

Banstead Urban District Council claimed in early March that everything possible had been done to keep traffic moving on roads, and that 900 tons of grit had been used.

In more rural parts of the county, snowdrifts blocked roads, and on the highest parts of the downs the snow was waist deep. In the Reigate borough, motorists were seen venturing out with snow chains fixed to their wheels. Snowploughs cleared Cronks Hill, Meadvale, the main route over Reigate Hill and roads near Gatton.

The Tandridge district was gripped by Jack Frost just as viciously as the boroughs bordering the London suburbs. Heavy snowfalls reduced attendance to below 50 per cent at Dormansland School, and 'owing to the inclement weather, the

The Hurst Service Station at Molesey was just one victim of the melting snows in March 1947.

Dormansland vicar, Rev E. A. Shattock, found himself conducting the evening service on Sunday for members of the church choir only'.

On 29th and 30th January, the thermometer read just 8F (-13C) at the Tudor House, Oxted.

TEMPERATURES AT REDHILL ON THE COLDEST NIGHT OF THE TWENTIETH CENTURY 23rd-24th February 1947.

Time	*Temperature* F	(C)
6.30pm	**18**	(-8)
7.30pm	**15**	(-9)
10.00pm	**9**	(-13)
Night min.	**1**	(-17)
8.15pm	**6**	(-14)
9.00pm	**13**	(-11)
10.45pm	**27**	(-3)

The longest period of continuous frost experienced in February for 106 years was registered on 24th February 1947. It brought to an end 14 days of continuous sub-zero conditions on the hills near Croydon. Not since 1841, had there been such a prolonged spell in February. On the night of 23rd/24th February, Redhill recorded 1F (-17C), a figure not surpassed in any future severe cold spell. On the same night, it fell to 14F (-10C) at Kew, and to 6F (-14C) at Greenwich. No wonder masses of ice floes were seen in the sea by hundreds of sightseers at Whitstable, Kent.

At Tatsfield and Chelsham, a bulldozer was commissioned to 'force a passage through the downs' while 130 council workmen battled with lorries and shovels to clear the deep drifts. Some villagers tried out a new motor-driven hand plough to clear pavements.

Where the snow did melt, there were reports of flooding. Ceilings were brought down by the weight of water which had got in after adjacent enemy action during the war. But for the Salfords Scouts, the only way to obtain water in the Ashdown Forest was to melt snow in a dixie to make tea.

There were some unusual scenes during the snowy spell. A swan landed during a football match on Reigate Heath and nibbled grass showing through the snow on the touchlines, and townsfolk in Reigate were delighted to see a horse-drawn sleigh that Mr and Mrs Robert Sanet of Monks Court Hotel used for shopping trips.

At the beginning of March, the Surrey Mirror at Redhill reported how, 'the continuance of the severe weather has been a trial to all and sundry'. People had hoped that March would bring relief from the ordeal, but the reverse happened. There were new snowstorms and more frost. Kew had 27 successive nights of frost from 11th February to 9th March. And on 4th March, an almighty blizzard hit East London, the snow being so heavy at Barking that, 'it was difficult to breathe or see'. Surrey escaped the worst of the snow that day but north easterly gales added to the chill as sleet and snow swept down. It was not until 16th that the last of the snow disappeared from lawns at Redhill when the temperature soared to 54F (12C) as areas of low pressure crossed the South drawing up warmer air from the Atlantic.

Roads turned to rivers and Summer Lane, Thames Ditton (above), was awash in March 1947.

Mayhem As The Snows Melted

March 1947

On 16th March 1947, mild air pushed into the country, as gale force south westerly winds buffeted Surrey, quickly thawing the last remaining patches of snow on lawns. But far from bringing an end to the weeks of inconvenience suffered during the bitter spell, the March winds brought with them heavy rain from the Atlantic, which, combined with the huge quantities of melted snow, brought havoc to towns near the Thames.

On 19th March, the Surrey Comet reported how the gales and heavy rain which followed last Saturday's blizzard, 'brought flood conditions unequalled for over 50 years.' The newspaper went on to say, 'Thousands of people have had to be evacuated from riverside dwellings. Sunbury, Ditton and Walton councils have opened rest centres for the flood homeless.'

By the night of Monday 17th March, the rising Thames threatened the huge pumping station at Hampton which supplies two million Londoners and most of the district. Two platoons of Coldstream Guards were rushed to the works to build parapets to keep the water from the filter beds.

At Walton Bridge, the Thames, 'overflowed its

banks to a width of a mile,' and in Molesey, supplies of milk and bread were brought to residents by a punt ferry service. Evacuation of Thames Ditton Island was in full force by Sunday 16th March and 'there was a big exodus to the mainland'. The rampaging river was not far from the Thames Ditton High Street and broke into the Home of Compassion.

Large scale evacuations from low-lying bungalows took place as water from the swollen Thames, Mole and Ember gushed into homes. Families carrying hurriedly-packed bedding and clothing tramped through the streets to find shelter. Thames Ditton's youth centre, village hall and church room were opened as relief centres due to the foresight of vicar Reverend R. H. Wilds. The WVRS served hot soup and made arrangements for stricken families. Marooned residents of the Palace estate were rescued by punt and taken to Hampton Court Way. One woman sat up all night with baby in her arms until the waters swirled around her chair. Many were reluctant to leave their homes and crouched on tables.

Some did not realise what had happened until they stepped from their beds into three feet of flood water. One family woke at 2.30am and quickly carried their four children to safety. They spent the early hours walking the streets and in the waiting room at Hampton Court Station before going to a rest centre.

At Walton on Thames, there were some dramatic moments. After spending five hours during Sunday night's storm perched in a tree near Walton Bridge, with flood waters swirling all around them, Mr and Mrs John Stafford from Shepperton were rescued at 2.30am and taken to Walton Hospital suffering from exposure.

They had spent the day helping neighbours to evacuate before leaving their own bungalow at 8.00pm. Before they could get clear of the floods, their punt was overturned by the force of current and they were swept against a tree into which they managed to haul themselves. Their survival instincts manifested themselves, and they shouted and lit matches to draw attention. Eventually, they were picked up in the headlamps of a police car and brought to dry land in a rowing boat.

At Sunbury, the Salvation Army housed evacuated families in huts at Thames Street and the British Restaurant staff stood by to provide food. The Food Office, set up in the war, issued emergency ration cards.

The Chertsey Road was under one and a half feet of water near Walton Bridge and the floods were said to be crossing the fields at a rate of three or four knots. Two lightweight bungalows were completely overturned by the raging torrents by the bridge, and at Shepperton War Memorial, the water was thigh deep. An Army Dukw delivered food supplies to isolated families in Ferry Lane, Shepperton, but two people trying to escape from their homes fell into the thrusting waters. Fortunately they were saved.

After the momentous weather in January, February and March, 1947, the following summer, as if to redress the balance, was gloriously sunny, and August was among the top three hottest Augusts this century.

Freezing in the Forties

1940 So cold in January that the Thames froze.

1941 Four inches of snow in early February at Redhill.

1942 Snow up to six inches deep in Redhill mid January and more accumulations in early February.

1944 Several inches of snow in Surrey either side of mid January.

1946 A freak hailstorm at Farnham on 3rd July. Hail the size of plums fell. Lightning set fire to the common near Ewshot gravel pits and windows were smashed in Farnham town. At Fairhaven terrace, Wrecclesham, almost every front bedroom window pane in the whole row of 20 houses was knocked out. Mrs G. H. Knight at No. 15 moved her daughter away from the window not a moment too soon, for just as she pulled the bedclothes over the two of them after a warning shout from her husband, the glass shattered and hail the size of mothballs fired into the room onto the bed and flooded the upper floor; the water cascading down the stairs. Six inches of floodwater swamped Castle Theatre and Norman Buckle and his wife 'donned bathing costumes to effect a clearance.' The storm knocked out over 350 telephone lines.

1947 The big freeze, during which the century's coldest night in Surrey was experienced. The temperature just outside Croydon fell to -1f (-19C). At Farnham, German prisoners of war were engaged in clearing the streets of ice and snow. Terrible flooding hit low-lying Surrey as the snows melted. On 16th July, Surrey's heaviest rainfall in three hours occurred. Five inches (125mms) fell at Wisley.

1948 At the end of February, 11 ins of snow lay.

A bus from Haslemere to Aldershot skidded in the snow at Longdown, Hindhead ,and its back hung over a 15ft bank. Efforts by the driver, conductor and passengers eventually got the bus back to the crown of the road, and it was able to proceed.

Odd Weather for the Time of Year

26th April 1950

Cuckoos were calling, nightingales were singing and there were flowers in profusion in every garden. The warm sunshine of Saturday 22nd April 1950 seemed to convince people that all in the garden was lovely and that spring had well and truly arrived.

It was with a little disbelief that people parted curtains on the following Tuesday morning in Haslemere and Hindhead to see a little snow on the lawns. But this was soon washed away by the April showers, and the Farnham Herald felt sure the heavy rain that night, 'would put an end to winter's nonsense.'

Not so. As a polar depression crossed over Surrey, tugging down Arctic air, the torrential rain turned to heavy snow in the small hours of Wednesday 26th April. With just five days to go before the start of May, snow lay on the ground to a depth of 10 inches at Churt, and dozens of roads were blocked and hundreds of trees weighed down and broken by the sheer weight of ice. Some 600 telegraph poles were either felled or snapped in two, and motor cars inching their way along hazardous roads became entangled in icy wires.

Buses skidded off snow-covered roads and in Farnham, the whole area was blacked out by power cuts. Farnham station was completely cut off, and passengers on a bus between Guildford and Cranleigh joined the conductor in helping to remove a tree which obstructed the way.

The snow caused such serious damage that questions were asked in the House of Commons. The Farnham Herald said gardens looked as if they had been under shellfire and remarked: ' The whitest Christmas Bing Crosby dreamed of could not have been whiter. Not a bird sang and not a flower was in sight.'

In the Guildford telephone region, bordered by Bagshot, Haslemere, Dorking, and Whitchurch, 11,000 phones were put out of order. 500 telephone engineers, backed up by crews from other parts of the country were out in force to restore supplies.

Hailstorm of the Century

5th September 1958

Giant hail as large as tennis-balls pummelled the earth; vivid blinding flashes and crackling thunder as if fired from a battery of machine-guns caused white-faced children to cling to parents. Grown-ups prayed and wondered if this was the end of the world. For many the evening of 5th September 1958 would never be forgotten in Surrey and Sussex.

The heaviest authenticated hailstones ever recorded in Britain fell that evening weighing 6¾ oz, and were the size of tennis balls just south of Horsham at Southwater. An airliner was badly damaged in flight near Gatwick. Roof tiles were broken, cars such as Morris Minors had roofs dented, and the ground was pitted to a depth of two inches. Tree bark was split open numerous windows shattered, and even lead frames were broken away. One woman was almost knocked out by a monster sized hailstone and needed several stitches in her head and was treated in Horsham Hospital.

A tornado cut a swathe of destruction as the storm intensified and beside the Crawley Road a row of cottages was almost demolished and trees torn out by their roots.

The storm moved on into Surrey. Cranleigh was on the edge of it yet manhole covers were forced high into the air by the flash floods. At Alfold, a garage employee waded thigh-deep into the swollen ink-black waters and then plunged in to attach a tow rope to a car which was literally afloat. Torrential rain inundated the Lingfield district. At Dormansland the garden of a Mr F. Adams was swept away leaving a five foot crater when a lake overflowed sending thousands of gallons of water hurtling down a hill. His attractive garden, a life time's work, was destroyed in seconds and to make matters worse his house was flooded too.

Such storms, being of the self-perpetuating, travelling type, often give heavy hail at the onset followed by rainfall of tropical intensity. As the storm moved north east into Kent, 5.14 inches (131mm) of rain fell in just two hours at Knockholt near the Surrey village of Tatsfield, this being the second heaviest two-hour rainfall ever recorded in Britain.

Even the north of Surrey was badly affected. Merstham and Hooley had 1½ inches (38mm) in just over an hour and it became pitch dark before a violent wind and heavy hail struck. Lightning damaged a house in Wallington almost blasting off completely the roof. The Wallington Civil Defence Unit helped the fire brigade erect a tarpauline to weatherproof the house. At the height of the storm, electricity failed in Carshalton adding to the terror of the night. One man was marooned in a telephone box surrounded by a raging torrent in Demesne Road, Wallington and was trapped until the waters subsided.

A train was struck as several thousand lightning flashes, some lasting two or three seconds, made this another serious contender for the storm of the century. Passengers were unhurt, but the driver suffered shock. The train which was slightly damaged, was taken out of service at Wallington.

1952 A violent thunderstorm stuck north Surrey at the end of August 1952. Hailstones, 'the size of mothballs', fell at Hampton Wick and a motorcyclist had the buttons ripped off his coat and his spectacles blown into the Thames. Mr R. H. Turk, the Kingston boatbuilder remarked at the time that, 'the tremendous wind seemed to bend poplar trees on the river bank almost double, and lifted Gridley Miskin's iron roof and stood it upright'. The hailstones were said to be 'inches in diameter'. At the height of the storm, the flagpole on top of St Mary's Church, Oatlands, Weybridge was struck, scattering large splinters of wood around, and lightning set fire to a tree in Monks Avenue, West Molesey. A man sheltering under a tree at Twickenham was killed. The brass plates under his cycling shoes acted as a conductor.

1954 A young man died at Long Ditton after the flooded Thames tossed a dinghy at high speed from The Swan, Thames Ditton towards Kingston in late November.

1955 Flooding again hit the headlines when the Mole and Ember swollen with melting snow and ice flooded 200 homes and marooned 300 more during January. Esher's Engineer, Mr C. G. Alderton, said the water was even higher than in 1947. One resident in Ember Lane, Esher, arrived homes to find her house swamped by 18 inches of floodwater.

An Alpine Winter

Big Freeze 1962-3

A pretty scene in Commonfield Road, Banstead, but the snow brought problems.

From a steel grey sky the first snow flakes fell, fluttering slowly earthwards in the still cold air. It was late afternoon on Boxing Day 1962. As the icy crystals gathered together in a steadily thickening mantle, it would be the last time the grass would be visible until early March. The Big Freeze had begun.

On Christmas Day a belt of rain and sleet moved south over Britain as mild air tried in vain to push away the cold continental air. Instead it turned to snow as it moved into the South-East. People leaving Richmond Theatre after a performance of Dick Whittington on Boxing Day afternoon were surprised to find their cars covered in snow.

Day-break on the 27th revealed a strangely muffled landscape heavily wrapped in a thick white blanket, eight inches deep in Redhill and 10 inches on the runway at Gatwick. The hills were the worst affected with the Godstone and Titsey area particularly difficult. Councils worked flat out from Farnham to Esher, the latter using 100 tons of salt and 200 tons of grit to keep the highways clear.

However, a worse foe was to strike. Gathering energy in the warmer waters off Cornwall, a deepening depression was heading towards southern districts armed with masses of fine crystalline snow and accompanied by a severe gale. During Saturday evening it struck and piled up immense drifts. Even main roads succumbed. The A246 Guildford to Leatherhead highway was blocked and so was the A3 at Hindhead as the wind constantly undid the work of the snow-clearing teams.

Country lanes were completely buried and one family at Beddlestead near the Kent and Surrey

A bulldozer from Upper Warlingham cuts a way through Chelsham in January 1963.

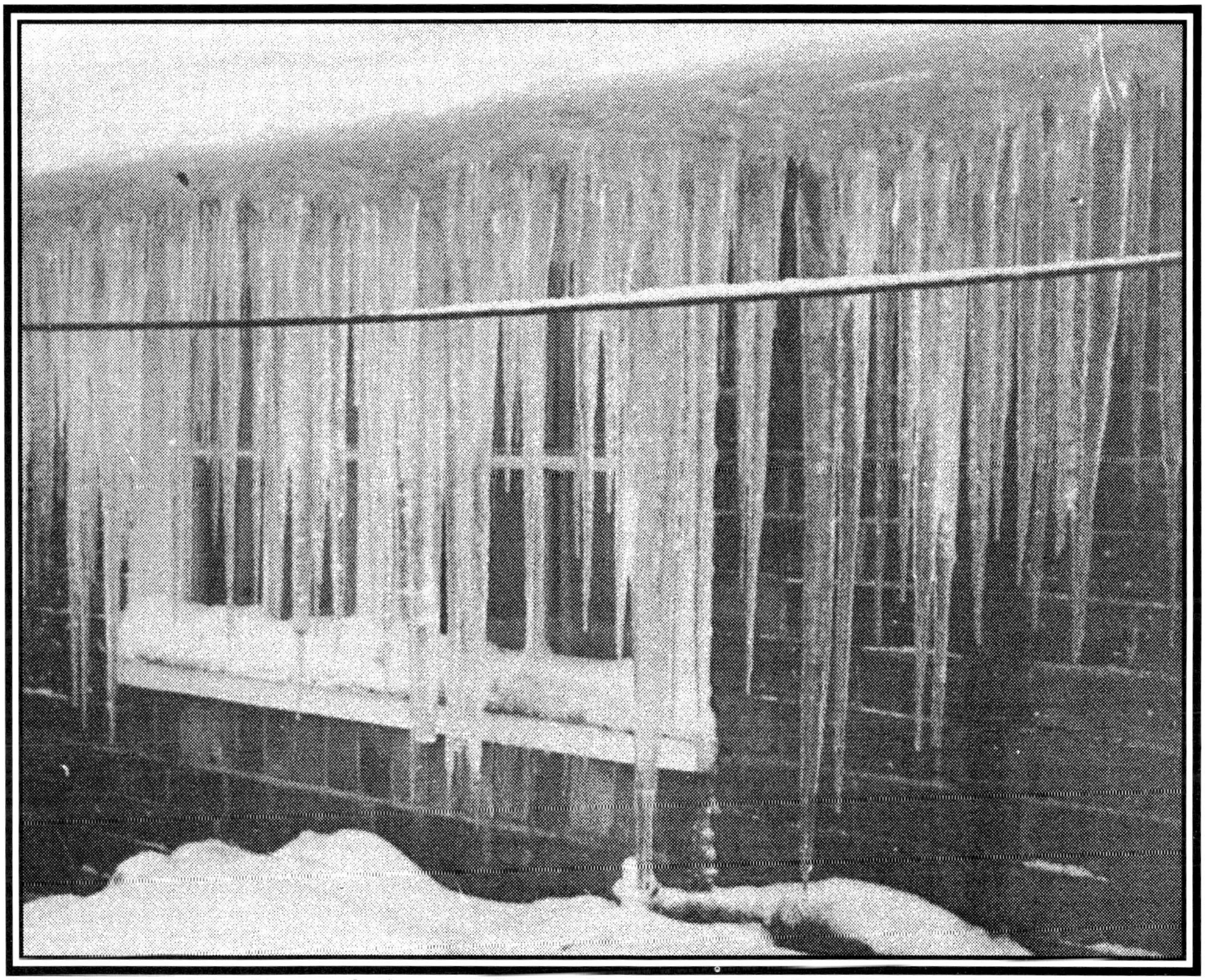

Icicles form a curtain of ice over bedroom windows in Josephine Avenue, Lower Kingswood in January 1963.

border was isolated for two weeks in their farm cottage. The Graham family's sole communication was a telephone link but that, too, was blown down several times. Mr Graham had an arduous journey through mountainous snowdrifts to the village of Tatsfield to buy supplies for his young family aged 15 months and one month. Their electricity supply was severed for a time and they had to do their cooking on an old-fashioned stove.

At the other end of the county the situation was just as bad. A doctor was called to a confinement at a remote dwelling between Bentley and Crondall near Farnham. Due to deep drifting snow she had to abandon her car two miles short and take to a tractor driven by the expectant mother's father, Mr John Inglish. He had never driven the machine before and whilst he gingerly operated the controls, the doctor was perched on top of a circular saw mounted on the rear of the vehicle in constant fear that he would press the wrong lever. Together they journeyed through snowbound lanes and fields before the tractor itself became firmly stuck with a mile still to go.

The doctor continued on foot trudging across icy terrain and arrived with just minutes to spare as Mrs Joan Marshall gave birth to a boy weighing 5lb 8oz.

Transport was seriously impeded across the county. Steam trains had to assist electric motor units on the Hampshire-Surrey border as conductor rails became choked with snow. Frozen points caused a derailment at Haslemere blocking both lines between Portsmouth and Waterloo. At Rowledge and Dockenfield, roads were impassable and buses stuck fast in snowdrifts. Some lanes near Peaslake remained closed until March.

It was particularly hazardous for snow clearing teams on the railways. At Farnham station with its 40 points and crossings, one linesman said that it was snowing so heavily that you could not see or hear

A Mr Thorn and Mr Mays celebrate the strength of the frozen Thames above Shepperton Weir in January 1963.

trains approaching and a lookout was posted. One false move and one could easily step on a live rail. Special ghost trains ran through the night coating rails with anti-freeze fluid.

In January alone, Surrey County Council used 2,000 tons of salt and 6,000 cubic yards of grit on roads, bringing together a team of 650 men, 70 snowploughs and 65 mechanical shovels costing in all £200,000. There was, however, a substantial drop in the number of deaths and injuries on Surrey's roads by some 60 people compared to the previous January.

The Guildford H Q of the AA reported 500 to 600 enquiries a day, many due to flat batteries. Even snowploughs were not immune to the conditions, for at Chipstead a machine became stuck fast and the crew had to spend the whole day digging it out. At nearby Mugswell two hundred people were isolated as winds gusted to 50 to 60 mph. In spite of this, bread deliveries were made by J. Lyons at Chessington where executive staff donned overcoats and helped bring loaves to Bookham, Effingham, Boxhill and Walton on the Hill, often walking long distances in the white fury.

The Thames froze at Hampton and on Garricks Eyot the Osborne family had to hack a path through the ice to open water in order to get their boat to the Middlesex bank so they could go shopping. The Hampton ferry-keeper also had problems and gave up exhausted and dejected after spending hours pounding the ice attempting to bring his cumbersome craft to the Surrey bank.

At Hampton, the temperature fell to 10F (-14C) and at Gatwick down to 3F (-16C). At Churt, the mercury fell to 5F (-15C) the lowest on records going back to 1941 and beating the previous lowest reading of 9F (-13C) on the 24th February 1947. January and February together were colder than at any time since 1740. Small wonder that the freeze took its toll on wildlife and led to stories of foxes coming out of the woods in the Thursley area to attack dogs and cats. There was even one report of a pack of ravenous foxes chasing a four foot high bullock at Boundless Farm into a ditch and tearing it to pieces.

Ducks were frozen out of their own home on Pirbright village pond and went to stay on a nearby farm to await the thaw.

An Arctic scene outside Watson's Stores, Horley, in January 1963.

Many outdoor jobs came to a halt. A hundred workmen including bricklayers and carpenters were laid off in the Farnham district and many a golfing professional was permanently 'in the rough', as many courses such as Hankley Common were unplayable since Christmas. One company, though, did beat the weather by constructing a giant 'cocoon' round a partially-completed block of flats at Ham near Richmond. Wates in association with Acrow Ltd erected scaffolding and then covered it with tough, transparent polythene sheeting. Work went on apace aided by heaters whilst blizzards raged outside.

The blocked weather pattern of the winter gradually eased. The westerlies returned and fortunately the thaw was gentle and not accompanied by heavy rain as in 1947, so flooding was not a problem. By 4th March the mercury stood at 50F (10C). Surrey was green again.

When the wind is in the East
Tis neither good for man nor beast

— Weather lore

The Thames at Shepperton under ice 7 inches thick in January 1963

The Warlingham area resembled a frozen wasteland in 1963.

The Surrey Mirror printed a souvenir card on the frozen Earlswood Lakes on 24th January 1963 to commemorate the unknown printer who on the same day in 1739 plyed his trade on the Thames ice.

Copies of the Surrey Mirror were taken by air from Gatwick Airport to rural communities in Hurst Green near Oxted during the severe weather in January 1963.

In commemoration of the unknown printer who on January 24th, 1739, plyed his trade on the frozen River Thames.

Printed by the Holmesdale Press Ltd., Redhill, on Earlswood Lakes, January 24th, 1963.

A replica of the commemorative card which was printed on the ice at Earlswood.

Siberia? No Surrey in 1963. Location: Chelsham

Memorable Weather In The Sixties

1960 A severe summer cloudburst struck Worcester Park, New Malden and Tolworth on Sunday 7th August. Shops all along Tolworth Broadway were under six inches of water. Only the bravest of drivers negotiated the sea of muddy water at Plough Green in Worcester Park, where 2.45 inches (62mms) fell. At Chessington, the 265 bus advertising 'Cerebos' salt 'made a wash like a liner' at the Bridge Road roundabout. Nurses had to be carried out of Tolworth Hospital 'by their menfolk'. The Kingston By-Pass was closed between Malden and Esher. In places floodwater was three feet deep on the A3.

In November, 1960, after 7.43 inches of rain in the preceding month, 7,300 million gallons of water surged down the Thames at Teddington in a day, compared to the normal 1,486 million. At Cheam, firemen from Sutton pumped away thousands of gallons of floodwater from Northey Avenue, and a night watchman from the council stood guard outside homes. On 6th December, 200 pupils at Sunnymead School, West Molesey, were sent home after water gushed into classrooms from the overflowing Mole.

1962 On New Year's Day, Redhill and Merstham were buried under seven inches of snow. Trolleybus services were badly hit in Surbiton and Kingston when heavy snow prevented staff from getting to Fulwell Garage in early January. Kingston Corporation were out in force, shovelling up snow and dumping it in the Thames. Homes in Ruxley Lane, Ewell had power cuts. The Metropolitan Water Board reported 550 burst mains. Esher Council sent out 15 lorries and 70 men to grit roads and clear footpaths. A bubble car overturned on Esher Road 'the new dual carriageway linking Esher and Hersham'. Winds said to have gusted to 75 mph blew over an elderly lady in Esher High Street. She suffered a cut nose.

In late February 1962, snow returned. In Teddington High Street, a skidding trolleybus driven by a Malden man, knocked over a passenger waiting at a bus stop. Two inches lay at Redhill on 27th February.

In May, ceilings collapsed in two houses in Ashridge Way, Sunbury, after they were struck by lightning. Mr Alan Wood, sleeping in an upstairs room was showered with falling plaster and glass. Milkman Keith Blackmore was pulling his all-metal float when he was hit. He keeled over after the shock, but later recovered.

December saw the worst blanket of smog for 10 years. It brought death, accidents and confusion to the Thames Valley. At Surbiton, it was so dense, taxi drivers gave up, and on 8th December Christmas shopping came to a halt. The Dittons had many power cuts. A man was discovered dead after being found in the fog in the doorway of Dorothy Perkins shop in Clarence Street, Kingston.

1962-3 Big Freeze

1964 In early June, lightning struck the Kingsnympton Park estate at Kingston Hill. An electric fire was blown out of the wall onto a settee.

Six cows were killed late in July 1964 when lightning struck a farm in Vale Road, Claygate. Farmer John Blake found the carcasses bunched together under a tree.

1965 A ferocious gale on Easter Saturday, 1965 caused £4,000 damage to a camping show at Sandown Park, Esher. Half of the 150 tents were blown down. Four people were injured and one was trapped. Many yachts capsized in an Easter regatta on the Thames and others were blown at 'an unprecedented speed towards the finishing line'. On Easter Monday it even snowed for a time. 'Hooligans who could find nothing better to do in Kingston on a bleak Easter Sunday evening pulled up tulip plants'.

1966 A severe gale in March 1966 brought down a 200 year-old cedar of Lebanon tree onto flats at the famous Pembroke Lodge in Richmond Park, causing thousands of pounds of damage. On 14th April heavy snow blanketed Surrey. Five inches lay at Redhill.

1968 Sahara dust coated cars with a coloured film on 1st July. The red, white and orange spots were attributed to high level winds carrying 'foreign bodies' from the Sahara desert. In September, thousands were homeless after devastating floods.

Wisley Tornado

21st July 1965

Students working in fruit fields at Wisley Gardens on 21st July 1965 noticed what they thought was a huge flock of birds in the vicinity of Ockham Mill, but what they actually saw was a tornado which struck at the Royal Horticultural Society gardens in mid afternoon.

The 'birds' were in fact countless pieces of twigs and leaves being swivelled around and upwards into black clouds in a giant funnel.

Branches were snatched from trees and torn like matchwood into a thousand pieces. The top of one large oak suddenly broke off completely and was carried upwards into the clouds. The same fate befell a hare unfortunate enough to be caught in the tornado's path – a hare-raising experience indeed.

The vortex appeared to have formed about a mile west of the gardens, near the River Wey and then travelled east to the fruit plantations on the edge of the RHS gardens. It swept through the fruit collection and continued over a short stretch of open land to the A3 London to Portsmouth Road. Ten trees lining the road were felled before the tornado then travelled a further short distance to Wisley airfield, where 'it did slight damage to the hangars before it died away'.

Some of those watching the tornado were frightened and ran for cover. The funnel took a zig-zag path as it ripped through the fruit fields, first passing near a damson field and then across a pear orchard. Fields were left in a state of devastation. So many apples were brought down that it was impossible to walk without treading on them, and whole trees lay with their roots in the air while full grown plum trees were demolished.

Altogether, 179 were uprooted, many beyond the possibility of being replanted. A further 56 were badly damaged or leaning.

It was reported that the whole of the fruit field area was littered with twigs of willow, cedar and ornamental oak which had presumably been carried a quarter of a mile or more from the garden at Ockham Mill and the river bank nearby.

Alongside the Portsmouth Road, forest trees with trunks six feet round were snapped in half. Several trees fell right across the A3. Two vehicles were trapped but no-one was seriously hurt.

One eye-witness, Jacqueline A. Radford wrote in the Royal Meteorological Society's magazine 'Weather'. She said, 'The storm was approaching

from the west-south-west and looked as if it would pass overhead.

'When it was very close with heavy rain falling, some low ragged fragments of cloud which looked like smoke, were observed moving in opposite directions.

'As they drew together and passed practically overhead, they were moving southward and appeared to be rotating. The rain had almost stopped and no particularly strong gusts of wind were noticed.

'A few seconds later a wall of very turbulent cloud moving eastwards appeared from behind a building about 300 yards south of the observation point. A funnel-shaped tail descended from it and there appeared to be debris drawn up into its wake. It continued to move eastwards and died out 12 minutes after it was first seen.'

The path of the damage appeared to vary from 30 feet to 100 feet wide.

On the day of the tornado there were two thunderstorms. One was at lunchtime and the other formed about 3 pm, causing 'spectators of the pruning demonstration to run for shelter.'

1969 Landing in thick fog at Gatwick Airport, a Boeing 707 of Ariana Afghan Airlines, crashed, killing 50 people. Visibility was down to just over 100 yards at the time of the collision on 5th January. An inquiry said that the crew seemed to have been searching for aerodrome lights rather than relying on their instruments.

The September 1968 Floods

Of all weather events that have hit the headlines, the devastating flooding in September 1968 must rank as the most serious natural disaster in Surrey, equalled only, perhaps, by the October 1987 'hurricane'. The unprecedented invasion of water into so many thousands of homes across the county caused so much distress and loss that even today, the year 1968 is synonymous with the word 'flood'.

Virtually every low-lying town was inundated by torrents of muddy water, which in places was so deep people had to move into upstairs rooms.

At Leigh, a woman was killed when her car was washed away in the River Mole and elsewhere, thousands were made homeless.

Evacuation centres were set up in many areas and the Army moved into beleagured towns to rescue the elderly and infirm from the rising torrents.

After a particularly cool, dull and damp summer, Surrey's suffering populace was hoping for some soft September sunshine. Instead some parts of the county received as much as a third of their annual rainfall in what was to prove to be the wettest September on record.

But it was the weekend of the 14th-15th that really made history. Torrential rain and thunderstorms led to widespread flooding compounded by the existing high moisture content of the soil. Some 2,400 square miles of the South East received in just 48 hours as much as 400 tons of water per acre with disastrous consequences for the Mole and Wey catchment areas.

The culprit was a rapidly deepening depression to the south west of Britain which produced a pronounced trough of low pressure across Surrey, along which there were large scale vertical motions of the atmosphere. Worse still, it remained stationary all day on the 15th. And that meant prolonged heavy rain.

The approach of the trough was heralded by a

With 10,000 homes flooded in the Elmbridge district and hundreds of roads submerged, traffic was turned away.

Drivers inch their way through the floods of September 1968 at Stamford Green, Epsom (left). In the background Christ Church can be seen.

Water cascades down a railway embankment at West Hill, Epsom, after the torrential rain in September 1968 (right).

Cars and traffic plough through the deep water on the A25 at Redhill Station in 1968 (left). On the right is the Odeon which in later years became Busbys nightclub and then The Millionaire. On 14th and 15th Redhill had a rainfall of 5.2ins (130mms).

The army and police row down Walton Road, Molesey, in search of victims.

The flooding at Old Esher Road, Hersham, was no obstacle for the most determined.

Pensioners are led to safety from their Molesey homes by the Army.

The half price sale at John Collier the tailors in Guildford High Street failed to draw the crowds in September 1968.

violent storm around lunch-time on Saturday 14th. That served to saturate the ground in preparation for the deluge to come. Later that evening the eastern horizon was lit up by frequent flashes of lightning. By midnight violent squalls buffeted eastern Surrey and continued almost unabated throughout Sunday.

Nowhere fared worse than East Molesey. Ironically rainfall here was *comparatively* low yet it stood square in the path of the accumulated floodwaters gathering upstream on the Mole. By Monday, East Molesey's main shopping street was a chest-high river of reeking muddy water. Upstream at Cobham the Mole was half a mile wide. The volume of water was a staggering four times greater than the previously highest recorded flood level attained in 1955. Raging waters swept away Downside bridge at Cobham and the A3 was blocked at Pains Hill. A vast lake formed between Hersham and Esher.

In the Walton and Esher districts alone, 10,000 homes were flooded. At Leatherhead, an estimated 1,072 million gallons of water poured through the town, and on the Sunday night a bus became stranded at Bridge Street and the occupants had to spend the night on the top deck before being rescued by boat.

Even normally placid streams such as the Hogsmill burst their banks and poured into houses. At Villiers Road, Kingston water was waist deep and in one house a brand new carpet was swept out into the back garden. The Pipp Brook in Dorking became a devastating torrent, tossing cars around like matchboxes.

For expectant mothers it was a particularly harrowing experience. In Thames Ditton, a mother-to-be had to be rescued by helicopter from

A canoe sets out in Cecil Road, Redhill, to offer assistance in September 1968.

the High Street and another was led to safety from Thorncroft Cottages, Leatherhead. Army helicopters swooped low over the rising waters directing rescuers to stranded people.

As dawn broke on Monday, the full extent of the catastrophe became clear. The whole of Molesey from Esher Station to Hurst Road and Hampton Court was under water. Boats were used to pick up distraught blanket-clad victims and ferry them to emergency centres such as St. George's Hall, Esher. The mounted police training centre at Imbercourt found itself the centre of operations with convoys of army lorries bringing sand bags and blankets. Amphibious vehicles were needed and two were used to evacuate scores of people at Byfleet where the River Wey burst its banks. Residents had to flee the Weymede Estate.

An estimated one thousand million tonnes of water fell on South-East England and much of this surged down the river courses. At Hersham on the Monday morning, commuters left for work armed with customary umbrellas but they were ineffective when they arrived back in the evening. A boat would have been more useful as they waded home, for the rolling tide of flood water had reached the lower course of the Mole and spilled out onto its former flood plain now mantled with twentieth century suburban development. That night, residents went to bed with barricades of cushions, old curtains, towels and plastic bags against their doors.

For some, next morning brought relief as the floodwaters had avoided their homes whilst others found carpets caked in slime, furniture ruined and even swarms of rats scurrying about. At Hersham railway bridge the water surged six feet deep and at Field Common caravans were floating in the murky mire.

The floodwater swept onto the Thames itself and at Sunbury the river overflowed its banks and tore boats from their moorings. Monday night was frequently punctuated by the eerie sound of vessels crashing against the weir.

Such times of adversity can bring out the best in people. Operation 'pinta' was launched and took the form of Jobs dairy roundsmen wading knee-deep or

A 119 bus destined for West Croydon hits floodwater at Bromley on the way to Shirley.

If it wasn't for the red phone box, it could be Venice. In reality it was Walton Road, East Molesey.

even rowing to stricken homes on the Molesey bank of the Thames. Local supermarkets gave out free food, and blankets were distributed to all who needed them in Molesey. Supplies of antiseptic and disinfectant were rushed from a Newcastle factory to the disaster area. Solid fuel was donated to help dry out homes as well as giant air dryers from the RAF. The Women's Royal Voluntary Service swung into action and provided a never-ending supply of tea and hot food in their makeshift rest centre at the Playhouse, Walton. This was much needed as many homes were without electricity.

The Services were mobilised, army amphibious dukws chugged along streets with personnel throwing loaves of bread into upstairs windows for the residents who had advice to quit their homes. Firemen worked unceasingly, pumping out water that still lay beneath floorboards even after the main flood waters had receded. Frantic efforts were made to extricate rotting food from shops and households by teams of refuse collectors, while the Red Cross and the St. John Ambulance gave medical advice and practical help. A mountain of ruined furniture was collected at Island Farm Road, West Molesey and bulldozers piled earth on top.

One local firm came to the rescue in a somewhat unusual way when they learnt that one of their employees would have to cancel her wedding reception. The venue, King George's Hall, Esher, had been commandeered as an emergency centre, so Bayer Products at Winthrop House, Surbiton switched it to their staff canteen. There was also concern about the wedding cake which was rumoured to have floated from the baker's in Thames Ditton but the bride's dress remained dry in spite of two feet of floodwater in the house.

Further west at Guildford, conditions were just as bad. The recently-built Yvonne Arnaud theatre was rendered out of action for several weeks by the untimely entry of three feet of water. Shops in the lower High Street area were flooded to a depth of eight feet at Millbrook with thousands of pounds worth of damage to stock. A bridge on the A281 Horsham to Guildford road was washed away at Shalford and the main Waterloo-Portsmouth railway line was severed by a collapsed bridge at Godalming.

Just across the Surrey-Kent boundary at Edenbridge, the town was cut in two by floodwater which reached the ceilings of some low-lying cottages. About 70 people were evacuated and because of a lack of communications between the divided parts of the town, there was anxiety over missing persons. A local mother whose daughter went to fetch a Sunday morning paper was not heard of again that day. About 80 rail passengers were stranded at Edenbridge Station for about nine hours before they could continue their journey.

In many parts a lack of news about relatives and loved ones was very distressing. Well over 10,000 telephones were out of action in the Molesey, Hampton and Dittons area alone. Kingston police

Oxted Fire Station was in need of a pumping appliance but crews still managed to turn out for emergencies.

The A25 was turned into a deep lake at Oxted and stranded cars nearly vanished.

station received thousands of calls from all over Britain as information was sought by anxious relatives.

The aftermath of such a flood – when the waters roll back and the reality and scale of the event sink in – are often the most painful. Infestation by ants and centipedes, huge growths of mould and the overbearing stench that such inundations bring, exacerbate material loss. Volunteers scrubbed the houses of pensioners but for many it was a long and uncomfortable process of recovery with houses bereft of carpets and fittings for many months afterwards.

Inevitably as the waters receded there began a growing storm of protest as to the lack of flood precautions. Why were the Zenith Mills sluices on the Ember not fully opened? Why did the weathermen fail to predict the storms? But the truth was that no-one could have expected such a widespread and heavy fall of rain.

A scheme designed after the 1955 deluge was effective until the extraordinary conditions of mid-September 1968. One could also cite the increasing urbanisation of the upper Mole's headwaters leading to greater run-off but as Esher's Engineer and Surveyor, Mr Kavanagh, stated at the time, "conditions were so freakish no arrangement could have avoided the catastrophe which hit the Molesey and Walton areas". Perhaps the weather could have been kinder in not striking on a Sunday when many council and river authority staff were off duty.

The violent rainstorm was responsible for a landslide at Pebble Hill, Betchworth, late on the Sunday night. An avalanche of trees, mud and debris hit a minibus, rolling it over three times and injuring the driver. He was taken to Redhill Hospital whilst the road remained blocked for over 24 hours.

One of the worst tragedies in the whole event unfolded on the Dean Oak Bridge near Leigh. Mr and Mrs Ware were driving across the flooded bridge when their car stalled. In the rear passenger seat was Mrs Ada Brown aged 67. In a horrifying few seconds the bridge collapsed and they were flung into the surging flood. Mr Ware escaped from the vehicle and managed to drag his wife free but was unable to release 18 stone Mrs Brown, his wife's grandmother. The car was swallowed up by the waters and it was not until the following day that Mrs Brown's body was recovered 200 yards downstream in 15 feet of water.

Lingfield was entirely isolated and in the surrounding fields and meadows much livestock succombed to the angry waters. Police using farm tractors and dinghies, assisted by the Army in military vehicles, visited the worst spots. Sightless and wheelchair-bound Miss Margot Godfrey decided to stay put in Yew Tree Cottage, Dormansland, with her dog and familiar surroundings. But outside her home an army lorry from Uckfield broke down and

Avern Road, East Molesey on 17th September 1968.

had to be towed away. Switchboard operators at Lingfield Telephone Exchange kept in close contact with her throughout the crisis.

Special driers from the R.A.F. were used to relieve difficult conditions in Station Road, Lingfield, and oil-driven fan heaters were on loan from Biggin Hill. A fire engine from Reigate was called to a blaze at a semi detached house in Green Lane, Godalming, because there was no appliance available at Guildford, Cranleigh or Godalming. A burning settee quickly took hold and it soon enveloped the house in smoke and flames. The Reigate firemen on arrival could merely damp down the gutted house.

It was a miracle that the fire engine managed to find a route through the floodwaters. On the Betchworth side of the Buckland Bends not far from Reigate town centre, flooding caused a seven-mile tailback of traffic and there was a four mile queue at Salfords on the A23. About 350 motorists were stranded in the Sidlow Bridge area and spent the night at High Trees School and Sidlow Bridge W.I. headquarters.

It was also in the Reigate area that two brothers saw a car topple over in floodwater in Lonesome Lane. Two children were thrown clear and stood immersed up to their necks in the chilly current whilst the driver, a non-swimmer, clung to the roof. Roger Portch dived into the rising waters and rescued the children and then the driver. Moments later the car was swept away.

At Redhill, a landslide demolished part of the Noakes family's home in Garlands Road, while police waded up to their waists in Cecil Road to rescue elderly people from their homes.

More than 400 houses were flooded at Cranleigh and conditions were so bad that 50 people were stranded on Sunday night and many local people provided food and blankets for the Emergency Centre based at the Church Hall.

An ongoing scheme to prevent another flood nightmare was quickly formulated and in the years following a new channel had been built to the Thames with the Ember taking the greater capacity. In all, some £19 million was spent with the works finally completed in 1990.

LEATHERHEAD ADVERTISER
BOOKHAM, FETCHAM AND ASHTEAD ADVERTISER
COBHAM ADVERTISER AND COUNTY POST
Your LOCAL paper
FRIDAY, SEPTEMBER 20, 1968

NOW WE COUNT THE COST OF FLOODING
Homes ruined, roads blocked

FLOODS which engulfed the district at the beginning of this week were the worst in living memory. Leatherhead Council have estimated that about 1,072 million gallons of water poured through the town during the worst of the flood, engulfing homes and disrupting traffic in two days of disaster.

Computer training planned for disabled

Front page of the Leatherhead Advertiser of Friday 20th September 1968.

SURREY MIRROR
& COUNTY POST incorporating the REIGATE BOROUGH ADVERTISER
FRIDAY, SEPTEMBER 20, 1968
Price 6d

5 INCHES OF RAIN—AND MORE LAKES THAN THE LAKE DIS

It all came in 48 hours, and these pictures show some of the trouble it caused. A woman died when a bridge collapsed, dropping her car into a flooded stream.

A Garlands-road, Redhill, family had a narrow escape when a wall collapsed on their home as they were playing cards.

This is what floodwater's fury did to the bridge over the stream beneath Old Reigate-road, Betchworth.

How the Surrey Mirror reported the disaster on the same date.

Weather in the Seventies

Surely not in April! The year 1978 saw heavy snow on the night of the 10th with temperatures down to 27F (-3C) which caused icicles to form on this car in a Caterham street the following day.

1970 In February, police helped to dig out 14 cars trapped in 18 inch deep snow drifts at The Grandstand, Epsom Downs. The 25th December saw the first real white Christmas Day since 1938 with six inches lying on the ground at Gatton Point, Redhill by Boxing Day.

1971 In May, lightning brought down a ceiling at a house in Court Crescent, Chessington, where seven-year-old Michelle Cordle was sleeping. She was treated at Kingston Hospital for shock.

1973 Disastrous cloudburst over Tolworth and Hook on 6th July. Three hundred homes flooded.

1974 Gales in mid January brought a tree crashing down on a car in Chessington Road, West Ewell, seriously injuring a man from Worcester Park, and in February, 70 mph gusts injured a man working on the roof of a building in Fairfield West, Kingston. He was put on a stretcher by firemen and lowered to an ambulance. In September, 60 mph gales blew down the marquee at the Molesey Hospital fete.

1975 A long hot summer actually began with an incredible sight – snow in June. Pupils at de Stafford School, Caterham looked out of the window on 2nd June to witness what their geography teacher told them was, "Something you may never see again in your lifetime".

1976 The famous summer with a long drought and water restrictions, followed a disastrous gale in early January which felled thousands of trees. People fled their homes in Spelthorne Grove, Sunbury when the gable ends of their blocks of flats collapsed. Police advised that they be put up in a community hall.

Several boats were adrift in the Thames, and at Giggs Hill Green, Thames Ditton and Weybridge, cars were crushed by fallen trees. Thirteen roads in Epsom and Ewell were blocked. Part of a house in Caverleigh Road, Worcester Park collapsed, and numerous trees fell at Kingswood and Tadworth.

The A243 Hook Road near Verona Drive after the storm.

Colossal Cloudburst at Hook

6th July 1973

One of the most remarkable storms in British history broke over Hook, near Chessington, on 6th July 1973.

At 5 pm, deathly black clouds gradually towered up in the warm but sunless afternoon sky.

As shops prepared to close after a busy day's trading, and those who had been on trips to the coast started their homeward journeys, a catastrophe struck the Greater London suburb.

The huge veil of darkness overhead, supporting such a fantastic quantity of rain and hail, could suddenly no longer carry its burden. The whole content was dropped at once - on one unfortunate neighbourhood.

So fierce was the rain that it fell like a wall of water and roads turned to rivers. Homes were swamped by muddy water up to five feet deep and windows were smashed by either hail or lightning.

The elderly in Vale Road South, Hook, were rescued in boats.

Within an hour, 300 homes were flooded. Furniture, coal and pets were thrust out of people's houses and gardens by the force of the water which in places was up to the armpits of rescuers. Elderly folk had to be helped into boats from upstairs windows and those who declined the offer were passed cups of tea on spades held high above the floodwater.

At Kelvin Grove, a prosperous cul-de-sac of detached homes near the Ace of Spades roundabout, a caravan was swept away and low-lying homes were under four feet and six inches of filthy water. Boats were launched in Kelvin Grove, Hook Road and Vale Road. In Woodstock Lane, cyclist Kevin Butler banged on a stranger's door begging for shelter.

Kingston Council estimated that 5.5 inches of rain fell in less than four hours - the equivalent of two months of normal rainfall. An official rainfall reading of 4.65 inches (118mms) was measured by a Meteorological Office observer, Mr Dowling, in Bolton Road, Chessington North, during a two and a half hour period.

Emergency services from all over South London and as far away as Bromley, Kent, moved into Hook to help. It took many hours before some fire engines arrived as traffic was at a complete standstill for miles around. People left their cars two miles away and walked home to discover the disaster which had hit their homes during the evening rush hour. One motorist took three hours to travel five miles, and when he arrived at Hook, he found roads impassable in all directions.

Police and firemen came under criticism for some of their actions, but they were only trying to do their job. Buses, including the 65 and 714 services were allowed through the deep floods in Hook Road near the Tolworth Brook, but this only created surges which further damaged people's gardens and homes.

Residents were annoyed, too, that firemen pumped water out of the A3 Hook Underpass which, they felt, should have been used as an emergency reservoir for the floodwater.

At Vale Road South, which in normal times is a row of Victorian terraced homes next to the trickling Tolworth Brook, elderly people were helped from their homes by rescuers wading waist deep into the torrents. Some of the victims were taken to an emergency evacuation centre set up at Shrewsbury House School in Long Ditton. Pensioner Miss Florrie Wiltshire said at the time, "I was in such a state I did not recognise anyone".

Firemen carried several elderly ladies to safety from their stricken homes in Hereford Way, while in nearby Clayton Road, shopkeepers Joan and Keith Easton, who ran the Little Shop, saw their rabbits floating down the garden on a piece of wood and along the road two chickens where drowned. In neighbouring Bramham Gardens, a plate glass window was smashed at the height of the storm and the road was soon under a foot of water which flowed downhill towards police-owned flats at St Paul's Close, and the Somerset Avenue estate. Mrs Jeanne Moore, warden of St Paul's church had to walk along walls in Clayton Road to get home.

Cyclists pedalling from Chessington Zoo to Hook battled against water in Cheshire Gardens half way up the wheels of their bikes for at least a quarter of a mile.

All houses away from higher ground were victims of the deluge and the shopping centre at Elm Road was flooded near the library and Hook Community Centre. The Lucky Rover public house had two feet of water in the bar area and the cellar was full up but it did not deter a customer from knocking at the door asking to be served.

Others were more concerned about the 'tidal' wave of water hurtling down the Hook Road from the North Star to the library, and worried about reports that a man had fallen down a manhole at Cecil Close.

The rain on 6th July was extremely local, but ranked at that time as the 24th heaviest downpour ever recorded anywhere in the UK in a three-hour period since 1900. In Surrey it was the heaviest downpour after Wisley's five inches (127mms) on 16th July 1947. While 4.65 inches was recorded at Chessington North, two inches (50mms) was recorded in a 45 minute period at Seething Wells, Surbiton. Kingston Council's engineer Mr Hugh Mitchell said, "This rainfall intensity is far in excess of that for which the surface water drainage system is designed, and which the watercourses and streams can accommodate without flooding. It was, in fact, outside the range of data of storms published by the Meteorological Office; was far in excess of the 1968 rainfalls and was probably equivalent to the type of freak storm occurring on average once in well over 100 years".

For most people, they had experienced a storm they were not likely to encounter again in their lifetimes.

Mrs Doris Corkran of Moor Lane, Chessington, and a neighbour were in Hook Post Office when the storm started. They splashed through the water cascading down Elm Road to get home and then offered a cup of tea on a spade to an elderly woman next door who was seeking shelter in an upstairs bedroom.

The vicar of St Paul's Church, Reverend Frank Giles, armed with flasks of hot soup, went out on a special mission. He offered the sustenance to one old lady in an upstairs bedroom of a cottage next to the Lucky Rover. She told him, "No thanks, vicar. I'm off to bed now and I won't worry about the flood until the morning."

In 1981, a major flood relief scheme got underway in Hook and Chessington, costing £1.75 million, but not before 30 homes in Cheshire Gardens and Mansfield Road were flooded again on 17th August 1977 during a fierce downpour. But after the 1973 storm, Kingston Council said that only increasing the size of drains seven-fold would prevent flooding after such a phenomenal downpour as that on 6th July.

Boats were used to help transport people through the terrible floods in Hook.

Troops, police and civilians were drafted in to try and control a huge forest fire between Tilford and Seale on 2nd July 1976. A square mile of trees became engulfed in the blaze and firemen from Farnham, Godalming and Haslemere were forced to retreat 'as trees burst into vast pillars of flames and smoke rolled across the forest in a smothering, choking blanket.'

Long Hot Summer of 1976

The sizzling summer of 1976 will be remembered as the year when water dried up, people were told to share baths, put a brick in the cistern and not to hose the garden.

It was also the year when much of Surrey's countryside went up in flames. Tinder dry heathland flared up as the strong relentless sunshine went on for weeks.

Between April and the middle of September, Surrey Fire Brigade answered more than 11,000 calls. So many that by the end of August, they had called in 22 of the Home Office's Green Goddess pumping appliances to help them out.

But with 200 calls a day jamming the switchboard at the fire Brigade's headquarters in Reigate, even with the best will in the world, not all calls could be answered. A woman who dialled 999 when a woodland fire flared up at Littleworth Common, Claygate, was told the Fire Brigade could not attend.

Eventually, a team of trainee firemen from Reigate pulled up - 45 minutes after Mrs Meg Davidson first raised the alarm.

On Wednesday 30th June, the day of the Littleworth Common fire, diesel drums exploded in an extensive forest fire at Esher Common which threatened homes. A police helicopter from Buckinghamshire circled overhead watching the path of the fire and contractors working on the Cobham by-pass used bulldozers to make fire

This may resemble a stampede in the hot and dusty Wild West but in fact the cattle are just following a trailer of straw at Greenacres Farm, Thursley, near Hindhead, in August 1976.

breaks. Later, at Surbiton, fire crews from Wallington hosed down five acres of blazing grass at Lower Marsh Lane which led to a huge pall of smoke hanging over Kingston and Surbiton. That night, 10 acres of grass and shrubs were destroyed at Warren Cutting, Kingston Hill.

All summer wide areas of Hankley Common at Tilford were ravaged by forest and heather fires. The situation became disastrous when a railway grass fire spread to a house and warehouse in The Fairfield, Farnham. Scores of Army personnel were called in to fight the seemingly unstoppable number of countryside fires in Surrey.

Waverley Council revealed that two thirds of the 1,400 acres of commonland at Elstead and Thursley had been affected by fire, and that two thirds of Thursley Nature Reserve had been wiped out. On Tuesday, 7th July, 50 paratroopers from Aldershot joined firemen and police in fighting a forest inferno which swept across a square mile of land between Littleworth Cross, Seale, and Culverswell Hill, Tilford. Residents were evacuated as flames threatened their homes.

Firemen under the command of Assistant Divisional Officer Edward Dunne and 20 policemen from Farnham and Godalming under Inspector David Stone, fought a desperate battle 'as it raced through the trees in a frightening wall of flame'. Troops under Captain Peter Morgan beat at the fringes of the fire, helped by residents and Forestry Commission staff. The Chief Constable of Surrey, Mr Peter Matthews and Chief Superintendent, David Eades from Farnham visited the scene. Mr Matthews praised the combined effort to quell the fire. "How tremendous it is to see the community responding to the crisis", he said.

Firemen from Farnham, Godalming and Haslemere were forced to retreat as trees burst into 'vast pillars of flame, and smoke rolled across the forest in a smothering, choking blanket'.

Miss E. Bell was asleep in her garden and was woken by a man and a girl to see flames and smoke sweeping down on her cottage. She was rescued and fortunately her home was saved from destruction. Three baby woodpeckers were snatched from the path of the blaze and cared for by a Puttenham resident.

Surrey Fire Brigade's Chief Officer appealed to Surrey residents to be patient in the 'unique conditions'. All fire calls were logged and some had to be dealt with when machines became available. Some, he confessed, had not been attended. On one day, 74 calls to the Reigate control room, which covers the whole county, were not responded to.

On 22nd August, one of the most serious countryside fires occurred in the South East when several square miles of commonland burned around the A287 Farnham to Odiham Road near Ewshot. Army bulldozers were brought in to make emergency fire breaks, and residents fled their homes. A reporter from the Farnham Herald surveyed the fire situation from the air after taking off in a light aircraft at Blackbushe. He wrote: 'It appeared in the clear conditions of an August afternoon that the whole of Surrey and Hampshire was alight. Smoke rose in columns from every direction, and over towards Bagshot a large fire was burning. The closed A287 took on the look of a dark winter's evening. Eerie figures could be seen beating at tongues of flames beneath the trees and choking smoke rose high above the Farnham skyline.'

Wildlife suffered badly in the heatwave. Smooth snakes, sand lizards, silver-studded blue butterflies and a variety of moths perished after the destruction of 900 acres of heathland at Pirbright and 42 fires on Chobham Common. Some adult birds fled their nests before flames got too close, but others stayed too long and died, the Surrey Naturalists Trust reported.

A Farnham vet reported that young dogs were suffering from heart problems brought on by the heat and that rabbits and guinea pigs were dying and aborting. People were suffering too. A Farnham firm, Martonair, introduced a new emergency timetable with workers arriving at 6 am and clocking off at 2 pm. They also ordered 10 kilos of salt tablets to help combat fainting among workers.

The heatwave brought some light hearted moments as well. Two small boys playing at Frensham Little Pond called the police when they discovered a 'body' in the lake. Police officers rowed out to find that the 'body' was, in fact, a rubber one thrown into the pond in 1969 during the filming of The Lost Valley starring Michael Caine. It had obviously re-emerged when the water level in the lake dropped by 27 inches during the drought.

Nearer London, the fire service was also put under immense strain. The London Fire Brigade's Croydon control, which covers an area south of the Thames down to the Surrey county border, answered a record 936 calls in 24 hours during the first week of July. A human chain fought a woodland blaze at the Shrublands estate, Shirley, on 7th July after the fire brigade did not arrive. Fourteen residents passed buckets of water along a line to put out the flames, and at Burgh Heath, plans were drawn up to form a village fire brigade, based at The Surrey Yeoman public house. As the crisis worsened, firefighters warned parents to keep their children off tinder-dry Mitcham Common, fearing that the youngsters would become trapped by fast-moving bush fires. Council workmen in Mitcham had to set up standpipes in the street to fight the scrub blazes.

Meanwhile, gardens shrivelled up after hose pipes were banned by the Thames Water Authority on 26th July. But Arthur Coast of Reigate devised a gadget to

The Chelsea Reservoir at Walton On Thames in October 1976 after the drought.

Year the river ran dry. This was the Mole at Young Street, Leatherhead, on 24th August 1976.

divert bath water onto vegetable plots by means of a nozzle fixed to overflow pipes. In Farnham, cows were fed on precious supplies of winter hay as grassland withered away in the dustbowl conditions.

Many local newspapers carried stories of water spies - people who had seen their neighbours and local sports clubs hosing down grassy areas for hours on end. Particular criticism was directed at Epsom Racecourse, where thousands of gallons were applied in preparation for the August Bank Holiday race meeting.

At Surbiton Lagoon, a record number of 5,600 people arrived on Sunday 27th June in a bid to cool down but the tragic side of the heatwave brought death to two Thames swimmers. A Croydon man disappeared while swimming near Hampton Court, and a Hampton boy of 15 drowned off the Molesey side of Platts Ait.

TOP TEMPERATURES IN 1976

Place	°F	(°C)	*Date*
Guildford	**95.6**	35.3	26th June
Walton on Thames	**95.6**	35.3	26th June
West Ewell	**95.0**	35.0	26th June
Sanderstead	**94.1**	34.5	26th June
Walton on Thames	**94.8**	34.9	3rd July
Morden	**94.6**	34.8	3rd July

- The hot spell was probably unprecedented in length and intensity since the 18th century. At Merstham, there were 16 days from 23rd June to 8th July above 80F (27C).
- At both Guildford and Kew, there were 38 days of absolute drought, and 36 at Epsom.
- Heathrow Airport had 52 days above 77F (25C) and 21 days above 86F (30C).
- At Kew, rainfall was only 58 per cent of the normal between July 1975 and August 1976.

A 65 bus destined for Chessington Zoo proceeds down the icy A243 at Hook on 31st December 1978.

The Winter of 1978-9

Frequent snow and frost brought misery to Surrey during the winter of discontent. People manning picket lines during the numerous industrial disputes felt the cold most as they huddled around bonfires to keep warm.

Average temperatures were up to eight degrees Fahrenheit below normal and in Redhill, January was the coldest month since 1963.

The worst weather arrived with a vengeance just after Christmas 1978. At 11 pm, on 30th December, a snowstorm accompanied by high winds, brought conditions similar to those seen on news bulletins showing adverse weather in the Scottish Highlands. A resident of Hook, near Surbiton, wrote: 'The Hook Road resembles that of a Scottish motorway on the news. Cars scarce; huge snowstorm and violent winds. People are staring out of the windows of the Lucky Rover, and two people with skates on, seen in Clayton Road. Neighbours are shovelling snow from side doors. Clouds of snow are being thrust off roofs by the icy gale.'

The blizzard brought in bitterly cold air from the east, where Norway was experiencing temperatures down to -40F (-40C); the coldest for many years. In Hook, the snow was falling at a temperature of 25F (-4C) and much drifting took place, both that night and the next day. The first day of 1979 was bitterly cold and sunny, and buses broke down on Reigate Hill. A sign outside Chessington North Station read: 'No more trains. All trains from Chessington *is* cancelled.'

Later in the winter, a 95 year-old died of hypothermia at her home in Headley Drive, Tadworth, and at Reigate, 21 buses were frozen solid. One bus that did venture out, hit a patch of ice and slid down the whole length of Cronks Hill at Meadvale. Some milder interludes did interfere with the grip of the icy spell, but blizzards were back in mid February, and snowploughs were seen on the M23. On 2nd May 1979, winter had one last fling. Two inches of snow lay at the top of Reigate Hill for a time, after a cold night with snow showers, and the sign to Merstham was obscured by icy slush. At Old Coulsdon tulips were weighed down by the weight of the snow.

When Day Became Night

6th August 1981

Night-time at noon - the A217 at Lower Kingswood around midday on 6th August 1981.

It was like the end of the world, black as midnight, ominously still, yet this was midday in high summer. A towering cumulo-nimbus or thunder cloud nearly eight miles high was passing over East Surrey on the 6th August 1981. Street lights went on and some people thought this was it - the end of the world.

Suddenly the storm burst asunder and lightning rent the sky. Bill Stevens of Portnalls Road, Coulsdon said it was the worst storm he had ever experienced. A keen gardener and sky watcher, he had known quite a few storms over the 50 years he had lived in the road.

In Surrey, 16 buildings were struck by lightning and the Fire Brigade received 338 distress calls. An expectant mother who was doing the washing up at her home in Manorwood Road, Purley, received burns to her hands and feet from a lightning strike as did an engineer at a Mitcham factory. Also three airport workers at Heathrow received injuries from a lightning flash.

In Waverly Road, Stoneleigh, lightning caused 20,000 worth of damage to a house. Even Sutton Police Station was not safe from the vicious lightning. At Addlestone there was a giant display of blinding blue light which was seen for miles as power from an electricity pylon short-circuited to the ground. At Coulsdon there were 600 peals of thunder including those from an earlier storm around 9 am.

There was widespread flooding. At Guildford the rain water was four feet deep and the AA Head quarters were put out of action. At Richmond Park Road, Kingston, children were using rowing boats and youths swam in Coombe Road. The Hogsmill river burst its banks and inundated Villiers Road swamping King Athelstan School. Purley and South Croydon were awash twice during the morning. At Burgh Heath, 2.72 ins (69 mms) of rain fell.

Shops were swimming with water near the Swan and Sugar Loaf, South Croydon after the storm of 6th August, 1981.

1983 July was the warmest month ever recorded since instrumental records started in the mid 17th century. At Guildford the temperature averaged 21C (70F).

1986 February was the second coldest this century behind 1947. It was so cold that the mercury did not rise above 3C (37F) at Tadworth all month and at Camberley snow lay for 23 days. In Earlswood, Redhill, a man went away for a holiday and returned to find the inside of his home entombed in ice after a pipe burst. Even the armchair and telephone were encased in ice.

The tail end of Hurricane Charlie washed out the August Bank Holiday with 1.6 in (41mm) of rain falling at Tadworth

September had the almost unique combination for an early autumn month of being dry, sunny yet cold. There were five ground frosts at the foot of Epsom Downs..

1987 January had the coldest day for at least a century. The 'hurricane' on 16th October is etched on everybody's minds.

1988 Parts of East Surrey had their wettest January on record with just under 8ins or (200mm) at Warlingham.

1989 The lowest air pressure recorded in Surrey since Christmas Day 1821 occurred on 25th February with a reading of 951.6 millibars (28.08 inches) at Horley.

A ferocious thunderstorm developed after a very hot morning on the 24th May when the temperature reached 82F (28C). A gigantic thunder cloud centred on the Mole Valley, and at Mickleham, near Dorking, 60mm (2.4 inches) cascaded down in just one hour. A truly remarkable fall. Guildford and Woking were particularly hit.

The 5th April was a unique day in parts of Surrey. The lowest day maximum temperature of the 'winter' occurred with heavy snow. The mercury climbed only a degree or two above freezing. At Hook, this was the first snow to have fallen since January 1987.

1990 After the Great Gale on 25th January, February was the mildest for several centuries and was more like that of Southern France or Italy. But 19F (-7C) occurred at Chipstead Valley on 5th April. After the summer's extreme heat and lack of rain, the Queen Mary's Reservoir at Staines was only 25 per cent full on 16th October. Another 'hurricane' predicted for October 30th gave just a light breeze.

Two snowy scenes from Dorking town centre on the morning of 11th December 1981.

Arctic Days in Dorking

The Winter of 1981-2

Despite talk of the 'greenhouse effect' warming up our planet, recent years have accommodated some vicious spells of cold weather. None have lasted as long as the big freezes in 1947 and 1963 but nonetheless, they have given us several periods of outstanding weather.

The winter of 1981-2 was particularly severe in early to mid December and again in early to mid January. As these two pictures taken in Dorking show, the first heavy snow arrived just after the morning rush hour on Tuesday 8th December and the hilly parts of Surrey by the following Sunday evening had nearly 12 inches (30cms) of level snow lying.

One hundred drivers were trapped in a blizzard at Epsom Downs on Sunday night, 13th December, and were forced to take refuge in the Berni Inn, Tattenham Corner.

The 12th December had dawned sunny, and there was an opalescent glow to the morning. It was a truly Alpine day and on Redhill Common, children enjoyed tobogganing parties throughout the afternoon. One of the most breathtaking sunsets ever known followed. A large rosy sun sank over the whitened slopes of Earlswood Common before the air turned outstandingly cold re-freezing the icicles hanging from shops. At Epsom Downs the mercury sank to 6F (-14.4C).

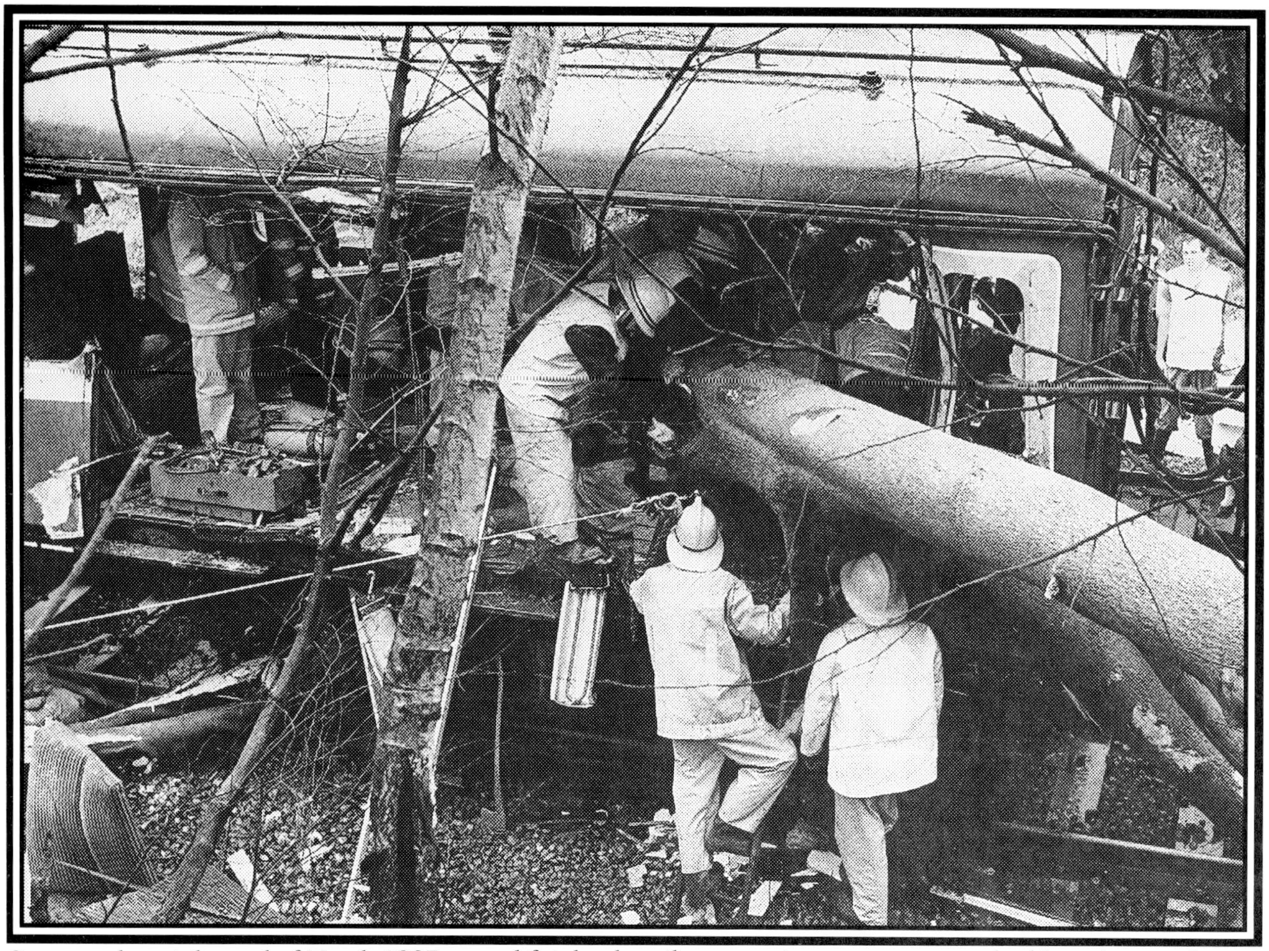

Severe gales at the end of March 1987 proved fatal, when three men in a van were crushed by a tree on the A217 at Lower Kingswood. At Dormansland Station (above), a tree speared into a carriage, trapping and injuring a male passenger.

Surrey Advertiser

Established 1864 — No. 14890 — Friday, May 26, 1989 — Price 22p

ROBERT DYAS
73 HIGH STREET
47 NORTH STREET
Tel. GUILDFORD 572826

● Pensioner dies ● Traffic halted ● Shops flooded ● Records go

Chaos reigns over storm-hit Surrey

AN elderly woman, known to be terrified of thunder and lightning, collapsed and died of a heart attack at her Guildford home during Wednesday's storms which brought the weeks of drought to a spectacular end.

Cool customers

Shops close as water pours in

SHOPPERS in Debenhams had to be hastily evacuated when flood water gushed into the basement from the underpass at the bottom of Guildford High Street.

WHEN this group of soldiers from Ash Vale took the afternoon off to go swimming, they didn't expect to take their dip in the middle of Woodbridge Road!

Instead of lounging by the Lido in their free time, they helped motorists who got stuck in a lake of water which formed outside Grays of Guildford when the storms hit the town.

The water, which was waist deep in places, covered both sides of the A25, causing traffic in the area to come to a virtual standstill.

Picture: Steve Porter.

Short-out causes spillage

THE lightning which accompanied Wednesday's torrential rain sparked off a major pollution alert.

Fires before the deluge

Weather breaks records

Angel struck

The front page of the Surrey Advertiser on 26th May 1989. A severe thunderstorm hit the town on 24th during which lightning struck the angel on top of the Guildford Cathedral tower.

SURREY MIRROR

Reigate and Redhill edition

No. 5755 — FRIDAY, JANUARY 23, 1987 — Telephone: Redhill 65431 — Price 18p

SOUVENIR FRONT PAGE TO MARK BIG FREEZE '87

ICE AGE 1987

Coldest day ever known

How Reigate shivered to a standstill

A souvenir edition of the Surrey Mirror went on sale at Earlswood Lakes in January 1987 to mark the big freeze. A similar ceremony was held in January 1963.

The Severe Cold, January 1987

The week beginning 12th January 1987 will be long remembered for its intense cold and deep snow which blew into mountainous drifts in the Surrey countryside.

Such a severe spell was virtually unprecedented this century, and rural villages such as Mogador, Mugswell and Tatsfield were cut off for almost a week. A Tadworth milkman went to hospital with frostbitten fingers while in Dorking and Reigate, some commuters headed to work on skis.

For the trickle of motorists who risked taking their cars out, journeys were harrowing. At Reigate Hill, the main A217 road was dwarfed to the size of a footpath by towering drifts, some 15 feet high. Through these, police guided drivers, one by one. It was even reported that flares were used to undertake the task, so severe was the blowing snow. At times, the visibility above the M25 was down to just a few inches.

In the shops, shelves lay bare after residents stripped them in an orgy of panic-buying, and at Woodhatch near Reigate, there was a report that shoppers had fought over the last available loaf of bread in the community's Co-op store.

At Coulsdon, the level depth of snow towards the top of Rickam Hill was 15 inches (38cms). Such a thick blanket of snow had not been known by Surrey's younger residents and probably equalled or even exceeded that deposited in the great 1927 blizzard.

East Surrey was, along with Kent, one of the worst affected areas of the country, being close to the North Sea. Clouds had formed over the water and built up huge burdens of snow which were readily deposited over the South East hills. But it was the intense cold that also vied for the headlines. Indeed, it had not been so icy by day since 1867, and considering the recent talk of a 'greenhouse effect', this was even more remarkable.

At Mickleham, near Dorking, on Monday 12th January, the temperature climbed to just 18.3F (-7.6C). And at Warlingham, Mr Tudor Hughes, a keen meteorologist, recorded a maximum temperature of just 15.6F (-9.2C). All this despite deep blue skies that day and bright sunshine. At Reigate, motorists had to scrape frost from the inside of car windows at lunchtime, and as soon as the scraper had shaved off the ice, it re-formed immediately in fern-like patterns. The only way to see out was to hold your breath.

The nights, too, were exceptionally cold, and if it were not for the passing snow showers, strong radiation into the atmosphere could have led to some all-time low temperatures. Even so, the mercury dipped to 3.6F (-15.8C) at Juniper Hall, Mickleham, on 13th and to 1F (-17C) in the Chipstead Valley near Kingswood late on 12th.

On Sunday 11th January, BBC weatherman John Kettley attempted to bring a little relief to his grim, week-long forecast. "The only bright spot on the weather chart is my tie," he said. There then followed a dire prognostication of heavy drifting snow and severe frost.

In the event, frost was continuous day and night between 12th and 18th in many parts of Surrey including Coulsdon and Epsom Downs. By Saturday 17th, ice floes were seen on the Thames at Sunbury and East Molesey - some of them eight feet across at

The Arctic conditions on Thursday 15th January 1987 hampered firemen trying to reach a blazing chapel in Camberley.
Wind-blown snow and icy roads made travel very difficult throughout the week and when the former WRAC College Chapel Hall caught fire off the Portsmouth Road at 4.30pm, severe problems were posed.
A fire engine from Chobham managed to get up the slithery slope leading to the burning building, but the crew were unable to tackle the flames by themselves. A radio message was put out for assistance but when supporting appliances arrived, they could not negotiate the incline until the driveway was gritted by Surrey Heath council.
The chapel was the only remaining building of the Royal Albert Orphanage built in 1864. It was gutted.
On the same night, two gritting lorries and snowploughs followed their tails around the A217 roundabout at Reigate Hill all night in a bid to keep transport moving.

Residents of snowbound Rickman Hill, Coulsdon, venture outside to fetch provisions on 14th January

Hampton Court where the river had frozen a third of the way across.

The freeze-up was caused by an area of high pressure situated over north west Sweden and central Norway. As a low pressure system over Spain moved north east into France, the icy blast intensified. Ferociously cold winds whipped up the snow into enormous drifts and blocked hundreds of roads. Meanwhile at Helsinki, the Finnish capital, the temperature had dropped to almost -40F (-40C) and had broken long-standing records. By the following week, a very gradual thaw set in, and very slowly the massive icicles on buildings started to drip and life began to return to normal. Unlike in 1927/8 there was no serious flooding when the snows melted, as the thaw was gentle and the weather dry. But in many houses, families had to spend hours mopping up when burst pipes manifested themselves. Water poured through ceilings and across roads which were found to be severely damaged by frost.

Snowdrifts at de Stafford School, Caterham, on 16th January 1987.

Banstead High Street on 14th January 1987 and Reigate Hill on the night of 15th January.

A sign of the times at Fetcham after the October 1987 hurricane.

Hurricane of October 1987

Winds exceeding 100 miles per hour caused the worst damage ever known to any living person in Surrey during the small hours of 16th October.

An estimated one and a half million trees were felled on that ferocious night in the county. A motorist died at South Croydon when a tree fell on his car and nationally, 19 people were killed.

The full story of this extraordinary night is told in the book, *Surrey In The Hurricane*, written by the authors of this book. It is published by Froglets Publications of Brasted Chart, Kent and contains more than 100 vivid pictures of the damage across Surrey and chapters are given to each region.

The storm is recognised as being the most severe since the hurricane in November 1703 and the devastation in Surrey's woodlands was unthinkable.

At Reigate Hill, thousands of trees planted to replace the magnificent beeches which fell in 1987 died because of the hot dry summers of 1989 and 1990. Some of the saplings were too exposed to survive because the hurricane had removed the mature trees which acted as a shelter.

The National Trust still had 10,000 trees to replant at Leith Hill in the autumn of 1990, and there was still work to be carried out at Limpsfield Chart despite the long hours put in by volunteers.

At the height of the 1987 storm, a landowner was badly burnt by his calor gas stove, lit in his home at Friday Street near Holmbury St Mary. It was many hours before villagers were able to get him to hospital on a makeshift stretcher by sawing their way through dozens of trees which blocked the roads.

In Caterham, members of the Cheshire Regiment decided to carry on camping. In the night, their tents were levered out of the ground by trees uprooting, but they somehow escaped injury.

The Great Gale 1990

25th January

The tremendous gale that caused so much destruction across Surrey on Thursday 25th January 1990 seemed inconceivable, coming so soon after the October 1987 'hurricane'.

No-one believed that winds of such violence would strike in Surrey again for many a decade. But while foresters and National Trust wardens were still clearing up after the 'storm of a lifetime' grim warnings were flashed on television screens as a ferocious area of low pressure looked set to unleash its pent-up fury over wide areas of England.

Savage winds increased in intensity throughout the day and by mid-afternoon, these reached speeds of more than 80 mph. Thousands of pounds worth of damage was caused in virtually every Surrey street; countless trees were toppled, roofs blown off, many roads blocked and because it struck during the day, unlike the last great gale, a number of people were killed.

A schoolgirl, aged 11 from Banstead, was one of the victims. She was crushed by a tree outside St Philomena's Convent in Carshalton at about 3.45pm and today her grave lies in All Saints Church in Banstead Village.

At Epsom Downs, a 75-year-old man was struggling to put up a rose trellis which had blown down, when he collapsed and died. It was the second tragedy in Epsom. A man in Woodlands road died after falling while trying to secure loose roof tiles.

In Haslemere, a man was crushed to death by a falling tree while trying to clear branches blown down in the gale.

Across Surrey, the damage in public places amounted to at least £5 million, the County Council reported. But while buildings could be reconstructed, the woodlands could not – at least for several decades.

One woman who was trapped for three hours in her crushed car on the Brighton Road at Tadworth,

A woman police officer picks her way through the debris in Ranmore Road, Dorking after the storm of January 1990.

survived, but was seriously injured. The main road between Sutton and Reigate was impassable and at the roundabout on top of Reigate Hill, a lorry balanced precariously over the M25. Two drivers at Bletchingley also narrowly missed death when their cars were tossed like Dinky toys into the bridge over the M23. Both vehicles were badly damaged and further accidents followed until police closed the bridge.

At Redhill, a tree smashed a bungalow in half at Kingfisher Drive, but the female occupant escaped injury. Horley was cut off from Redhill and a roof was blown off a house in Oakwood Road. Three planes were tipped over by winds which reached 83 mph at Gatwick Airport just after 1.30pm.

In Dorking, a gardener was trapped under a tree at the Friends Providence and was injured, but Mr Roger Cooke narrowly missed being hurt when his car was condensed by a falling tree at the Tyrells Wood Golf Course. The railway line between Dorking and Horsham was blocked for a whole day and Victoria was the only London station that remained open.

High up on the North Downs at Chelsham, a double decker bus was blown over, but luckily no-one was hurt.

At Stoneleigh near Epsom a chimney crashed through the window of Graeme Fuller Classic Cars. Vintage cars were slightly damaged, and a customer suffered cuts and needed hospital treatment.

Further north in Richmond, 300 trees were felled and many local residents were injured after being hurled to the ground. Valiant efforts by Richmond Council tree surgeon Andrew Pinder failed to save the life of an elderly man crushed in his car at Brinsworth Close, Twickenham. Television star Gorden Kaye from 'Allo 'Allo was critically injured when a wind-blown plank of wood pierced through his car windscreen and lodged into his head. He later recovered.

At Kew Gardens, 100 valuable trees were uprooted, including a rare Iron Tree from Persia,and the grounds had to be closed for a week.

Schoolchildren at Chessington were shepherded away from a playroom at Ellingham School seconds before a roof was blown off into the playground, and down the road at RAF Chessington, £20,000 worth of roofing panels were prised off 25 buildings.

New Malden's Green Theatre Company was forced to abandon its production of Grease after leading actor David Wheatley was struck on the head by a flying branch, and at Shannon Corner, two people were injured when a billboard fell on a car. The California Road resembled a demolition site, with four cars buried under a mountain of bricks.

In Kingston town centre, shoppers dodged death

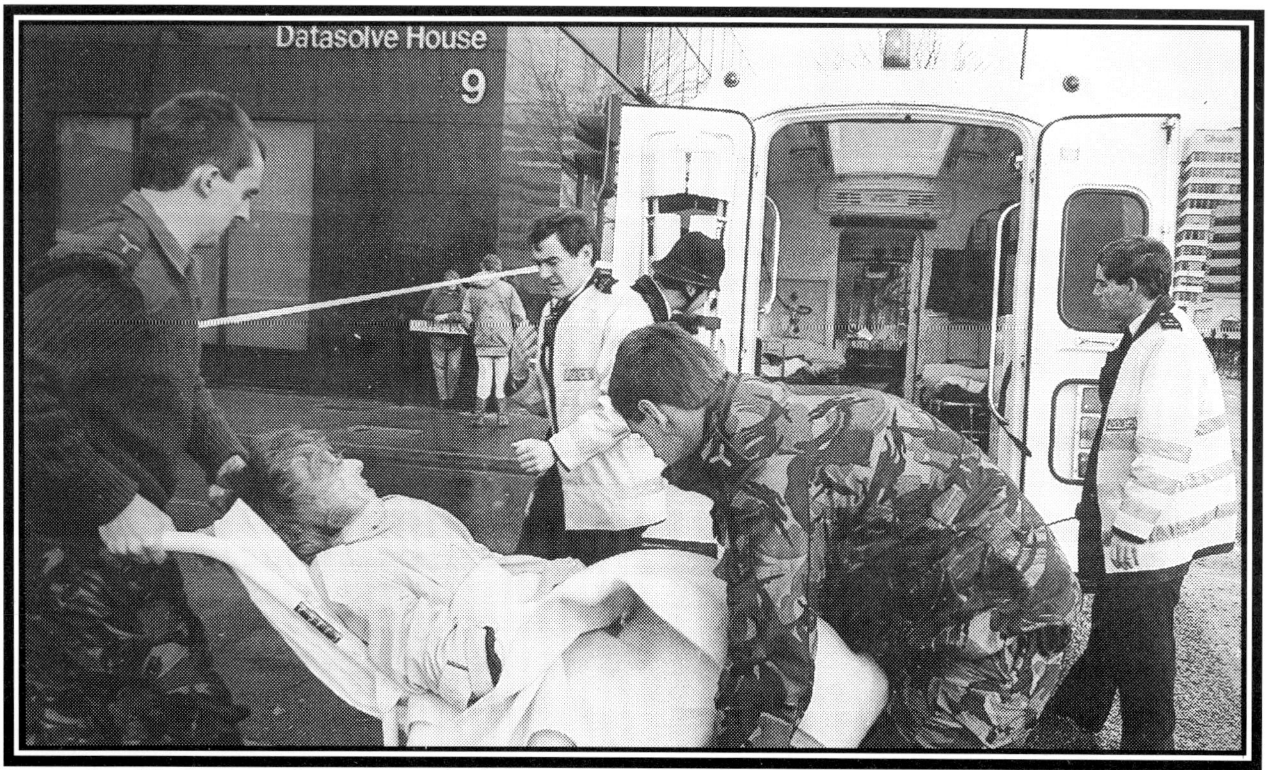

A casualty of the hurricane force winds at Sunbury is taken to hospital by Army personnel during the ambulance dispute.

A woman aged 74 had to crawl out of her crushed mobile home at Laleham Reach.

when an entire window and frame rained down onto the Eden Walk shopping precinct, and in Surbiton the main shopping street, Victoria Road, was roped off after part of the old Barclays Bank building collapsed.

Traffic was turned away from Richmond Park because of the dangers of trees falling and motorists thinking they were safe in built up areas found they were not out of the woods. At Hinchley Wood the roof of the Shell service station collapsed and led to the appearance of a bomb site.

Elmbridge Council estimated a clear-up bill of at least £½ million and said the storm was, 'every bit as bad', as in October 1987. The figure was chiefly made up of the large sums of money spent on all the heavy lifting gear, earth movers and lorries, ' needed to cope with the enormous amount of damage'.

Walton town hall received 200 calls from people in distress, and police were getting reports of damage occurring every four seconds. In Thames Ditton, seven roofs were blown off in Long Mead Road. Surrey Ambulance Service, in dispute at the time, forgot their grievances, and answered nearly 300 calls, some with assistance from the Army.

Tandridge District Council received 300 calls reporting damaged of some kind to council homes and properties. The Slines Oak area of Woldingham was badly hit with trees blocking roads and in one incident a man was trapped in his car. In another, the driver escaped.

At Walton, old people were evacuated from their flats at Mount Felix after a huge cedar burst into the building and at Longcross Road, Chertsey, occupants of a car were trapped when a tree fell on top of it. A house at Oxshott was sliced in two.

In the Sunbury area, high rise blocks acted like red rags to the wind which increased in intensity as if to prove that nothing could get in its way. Several pedestrians became airborne for a few moments and were hurt when dropped to the ground. A woman police officer was lifted off her feet and blown into the path of a car. She suffered back injuries and was therefore not able to help when another woman was tossed into a post and had to be taken to hospital on a stretcher. Debris was flying off the skyscrapers in all directions and roads underneath had to be shut. Elderly residents of Benwell House were evacuated after windows blew in.

Weybridge suffered just as much as everywhere else and in Brooklands Road, a woman was trapped in her car and was seriously injured after a tree fell.

In Croydon, which is windswept on the best of days, walking was made impossible, and the design of the tower blocks was blamed for causing wind tunnels through the town. 'People were hanging onto lamp posts and litter bins to avoid being bowled over or thrust into the passing traffic,' said the Croydon Advertiser. A bus was blown off course into railings, and the 18-storey Taberner House was evacuated when it began to sway.

Runnymead Council estimated the storm would leave a bill for £3 million and reported that the worst damage was in the Englefield Green and Virginia Water area where, in one incident, the roof of a mobile classroom at Trumps Hill First School blew off.

The Mitcham Herald told how 26 families had to be evacuated from their homes on the Laburnham Road estate when a chimney toppled. Five spent the night in the council's Woodlands Centre. Meanwhile, the 70 year-old steeple of St. Mark's Church crashed down and the vicar Rev. Peter Tilley was thankful to God that it had not fallen the other way - where 70 people were having lunch in the family centre.

In Guildford, a workman was injured and eight cars damaged when the Mann Egerton garage collapsed. Two children and a couple of cars were hit by a flying roof at Park Barn School and at the Bishop Reindorp school, the dry ski area was smashed to smithereens.

The rural villages around Guildford and Godalming were in darkness for several days and at Compton, families huddled around candles until power was restored. With many homes having no telephone link, it was a pretty primitive existence for a time. The Godalming area was equally affected and several cars parked outside the Inn on the Lake pub were beyond repair after a tree uprooted. At Milford, passengers had to walk along the track to reach the railway station after a tree blocked the line.

Wisley Gardens fell victim again, and one section had been open only 26 days following the 1987 storm, when the new damaged occurred.

In Farnham, a man died at the Guildford Road Industrial Site after he fell to his death trying to repair a hole torn in the roof of a warehouse by a fallen tree. A short drive away, at Frensham, firemen worked for two hours to free injured Mrs Jacqueline Paramor who was trapped in her car with a tree pinning it down. At Churt, a schoolgirl was hit on the head by a branch after fleeing from a car to escape from crashing trees.

Electricity workers were brought into West Surrey from Southern Ireland to help out during the crisis and restore power to homes. Surrey Fire Brigade answered 543 calls in a day.

Residents of Haslemere mourned the death of good neighbour Mr Derek Blake who was killed after he and neighbours tried to clear a tree which had fallen across Scotland's Lane. Suddenly a beech tree toppled and struck Mr Blake.

At Woking, the scene was strikingly similar to that in all Surrey towns. A window blew out of the Allied Carpets building and caused severe head injuries to a passerby.

Striking during the day, there were more casualties in this storm than in October 1987, which arrived in the dead of night, causing two fatalities in and around the county, but wiping out greater areas of woodland. The west of Surrey suffered more damage than in 1987 in some people's opinions.

There was no difference in the formation of both storms. Cold polar air clashing with warm air from southerly latitudes caused a sudden explosive deepening as the warm winds were flung rapidly aloft. A violent vortex resulted and it was sent whirling towards Britain in the strong jet stream or upper winds. The fact that the sea temperatures were some 4F (2C) above normal around the South Coast after the warm weather of 1989 gave an additional impetus to the low pressure system.

Global warming was blamed by some for the storm, and it is true that higher temperatures could lead to more violent tempests.

Nationally, the 1990 storm, together with the bad weather in the following five weeks, caused an estimated £2,500 million damage.

TEMPERATURES RECORDED IN THE GREAT HEAT

3rd August 1990

Place	*°F*	*°C*
GUILDFORD		
Sheepford Road (John Morris)	**97.7**	36.5
EPSOM		
Langley Vale (John Bird)	**96.8**	36.0
EWELL		
Castle Avenue (Peter Clarke)	**96.5**	35.8
SANDERSTEAD		
Shaw Crescent (Chris Elston)	**96.3**	35.7
REIGATE		
Woodhatch (Colin Finch)	**96.4**	35.8
GUILDFORD		
Onslow Village (Dennis Mullen)	**95.9**	35.5
SOUTH LONDON		
West Norwood	**95.5**	35.3
WALLINGTON		
Crichton Avenue (Mr Gait)	**95.0**	35.0
TADWORTH		
Acres Gardens (John Carter)	**95.0**	35.0
COULSDON		
Rickman Hill (Ian Currie)	**95.0**	35.0
GATWICK AIRPORT		
near Horley	**95.0**	35.0
WARLINGHAM		
Chapel Road (Rev. Michael David)	**94.3**	34.6
CATERHAM SCHOOL		
Harestone Valley Road	**94.1**	34.5
Average maximum in Surrey on 3rd August 1990	**95.7**	35.4

Burning Hot Summer 1990

After the ferocious storms earlier in the year, Surrey people deserved the reward of a sunny settled summer. But as temperatures soared into the upper nineties, this proved to be a blessing in disguise.

By early August, there was a widespread ban on the use of hosepipes in the Thames Water area and a sprinkler ban in other parts, and as reservoirs emptied, gardens turned brown and withered. Autumn-coloured leaves started falling in late July, ducks quit their village ponds and as heaths and commons dried in the hot sun, fires raged out of control.

Just like in 1976, snakes, lizards and birds were destroyed as vast areas of the Surrey countryside went up in smoke.

The most dramatic blaze broke out on the evening of Sunday 5th August when more than 250 acres of Ash Ranges were swept by a devastating fire which led to 20 people being evacuated from their homes on the Pirbright Road at Normandy. Firemen helped RSPCA officials carry 12 Rotweiller and Alsatian dogs to safety as thick smoke swirled around their kennels while residents further up Pirbright Road removed crates of racing pigeons to safety. It was so hot as the fire raged nearby that the dogs could not be shut up inside the house. Their owner could not open the windows because the choking smoke would have got inside.

People were taken to a community centre for the night as 100 firemen tackled the flames and civilians using bulldozers made fire breaks. Police sealed off parts of Ash, Pirbright and Normandy as the huge blaze spread. Score of people using binoculars watched from the Hogs Back ridge as a huge wall of flames fanned by a strong breeze swept northwards. At one stage it was so hot, trees were igniting before the flames reached them.

The smoke reached Epsom Downs 30 miles away and the glow could be seen from Leatherhead.

Two weeks earlier, another serious fire wiped out a square mile of Hankley Common near Elstead. A soldier battling with the blaze was taken to hospital at Aldershot suffering from heat exhaustion and hundreds of cartridges exploded in the heat near to the army training huts at the dropping zone.

In early August, massive fires destroyed many square miles of heathland at Deepcut and Bisley. More than 50 outbreaks of fire occurred at the Lightwater Country Park and the MoD woods at The Maultway, Camberley.

On 12th August, more than 30 acres of Chobham Common were damaged by fire, and 50 gipsies were evacuated from their caravans at Burma Road. Mr Alan Greenwood of Chobham, who collects vintage fire engines loaned his Dennis F24 appliance to firemen at the scene. A crew from Ascot directed its 400 gallons of water onto the blaze. The old machine was one of a batch supplied to Surrey Fire Brigade in 1960. Dozens of families were evacuated by police from another blaze the same day on Thursley Common near Hindhead.

The Brigade was so stretched on 12th August that a fire tender from Twickenham, Middlesex, was asked to man Camberley Fire Station. Days earlier, crews had been brought in from Portsmouth, Cosham and Southampton Water to cover Surrey's fire stations. More than 8,000 calls were received at the Brigade headquarters in Reigate during July and August.

At the Cranleigh Show on 4th August sand in the jumping rings saved horses from injury on rock hard ground, and goats were kept cool with makeshift showers. The traditional goat parade was cancelled because of the 93F heat.

Dozens of families cooled off during August by taking a dip in the shallow waters of the River Wey near the Barley Mow public house at Tilford and sweet shops throughout the county suffered as chocolate bars melted, but it was a successful year for the wasp population. St Helier Hospital near Carshalton treated 21 wasp-sting casualties in one weekend, when normally they deal with only one a day in the summer. And while London's Big Ben clock packed up in the heat on Thursday 2nd August, the same fate befell St Matthew's Church clock in Redhill. It chimed 11 times at 5am.

The heat also played havoc with the electricity. Buckled equipment is thought to have caused a huge power cut in Redhill and Meadvale on 4th August. British Rail was thrown into chaos when rail lines warped in the intense heat on inter city routes and a speed limit had to be imposed.

Farmers reported a poor yield of cereal crops on sandy soil sites around the county, but grapevines in Leatherhead and Dorking thrived. The heatwave was a disaster for fish in village ponds. Some were rescued by the National Rivers Authority but others, deprived of oxygen, died.

*This 1960 fire engine, pictured **above** at Esher when new, proved it still had a use in 1990 when it was brought out of mothballs to help tackle heathland fires at Horsell Common **(below)** and Chobham Common during the long hot summer. The old engine, owned by Mr Alan Greenwood of Chobham, has seen all weathers. In 1968, it was used solidly for a fortnight pumping out flooded homes around Esher, and in 1975 and 1976 it spent many long hours at countryside blazes during the drought conditions.*

Huge fires ripped through the tinder dry countryside at Deepcut and Ash Ranges in August 1990.

In July and August 1990, the Surrey countryside was at flashpoint. On 4th August Surrey Fire Brigade tackled 103 separate heath and grass fires in one day.

Crews worked exceptionally long hours but at one stage, the flames seemed to be winning. On Thursday 2nd August, Chobham's retained firemen started out at 8.20 am and after five incidents were called at 2.00 pm to an undergrowth blaze at Alma Gardens, Deepcut. Leading fireman Belcher radioed for extra help, but was told that no further fire engines were available. The crew 'lost' the fire after four hours to an Army restricted area, and by morning 12 fire engines were involved in bringing it under control.

The Chobham firefighters were eventually sent home at 2.55 am on Friday 3rd August after working for nearly 19 hours.

During the crisis it was not unusual to see fire engines from Oxted, Godstone and Lingfield, fighting blazes 40 miles away in Hindhead and Farnham.

The Farnham Herald warned villagers in Tilford of the dangers in the 1990 heatwave.

Kingfield Pond at Woking dried up for the first time in most people's memories during the summer of 1990. Here, Rowland Pallant of the Kingfield Conservation Group studies the cracks in the bed of the pond. Earlier, the National Rivers Authority came along and stunned dozens of ailing carp, golden rudd and tench before rescuing them. Forty mallard ducks made off for pastures new but the moorhens stayed put.

Swans normally glide over the water where these people are walking. But in September 1990 the water in West End pond, Esher, had completely dried up.

The summer of 1990, like 1989, was a great year for grapes, and vintage wine was plentiful at Headley Farm near Leatherhead, and on the slopes above Dorking. Pictured above is Guy Woodall of Leatherhead's Thorncroft Vineyard showing the bumper crop in 1990.

The slopes of Banstead Woods in the Chipstead Valley were descended on by winter sports enthusiasts in February 1991. The valley is one of the coldest spots in Southern England on clear calm nights.

A Remarkable Surrey Valley

The night was still. The snow lay crisp and frost covered. It crunched and crackled under foot. Clouds of steam rose from manhole covers along the road and my nostrils started to freeze; one of the perils of taking weather readings in the Chipstead Valley between Kingswood and Coulsdon. The time was 11pm and the mercury had sunk to 0F (–17.5C). The date was the 8th January 1985.

This well-known frosty valley traps cold air draining off the enclosing chalk hills. Its dry, gravelly floor permits rapid radiation and cooling and makes it a hazardous location for vegetable and fruit growers. It has recorded some unseasonal temperatures such as 29F (–2C) on the 2nd June 1991, with the temperature falling again below freezing on the 5th. And this North Downs valley is only five miles from Croydon's Manhattan-like centre.

In February 1991, the temperature plummetted to just 3F (–16C), the lowest in Britain that winter. However, for those who are resident in this polar-like valley, some comfort can be drawn from the fact that it is also a sun trap by day and on the 1st September 1991, a reading of 86F (30C) rivalled the Mediterranean resorts. — *Ian Currie.*

WEATHER DIARY FOR COLD SNAP FEBRUARY 1991 AT COULSDON

Date	*Conditions*	*Max F*	*(C)*	*Min F*	*(C)*	*Wind*
Mon 4th	Bright or sunny spells	35	(+1)	22	(–6)	Calm
Tue 5th	Light snow at times	33	(+0)	28	(–2)	NE
Wed 6th	Frequent snow showers	29	(–2)	27	(–3)	NE
Thu 7th	Heavy snow at times	23	(–5)	13	(–11)	N
Fri 8th	Snow, heavy at times	26	(–4)	19	(–7)	N
Sat 9th	Some heavy snow showers	26	(–4)	20	(–7)	N
Sun 10th	Snow showers	32	(–0)	16	(–9)	N
Mon 11th	Sunny periods	33	(+0)	21	(–6)	NW
Tue 12th	Heavy snow in evening	36	(+2)	23	(–5)	Calm
Wed 13th	Cloudy, slight snow am	35	(+2)	26	(–4)	N
Thu 14th	Sunny. Freezing fog am	38	(+3)	24	(–5)	NW

Readings taken at Rickman Hill, Coulsdon, half a mile from Chipstead Village. The maximum depth of snow was just over 9ins (23cms) on Wednesday 13th February. This compared with 15 ins (38 cms) in January 1987 – one of the heaviest falls of the 20th century. High on the North Downs at Warlingham, Mr Tudor Hughes recorded a maximum of 22F (–6C) on February 7th. The lack of serious drifting in February 1991 made the wintry weather less severe than in 1987.

The piste was good on Box Hill in February 1991 but the snow badly hampered trains.

The Wrong Type of Snow

February 1991

After a run of mild winters, Surrey children were over the moon when February 1991 brought snow so thick they were able to spend days going down hills on sledges, making snowmen and throwing snowballs.

A very cold pool of air over Scandinavia and north west Russia moved south-westwards in the first week of the month, heralding a fortnight of intense cold and much snow.

The snow was fine - like white sand - due to the temperature being below freezing, preventing it from clogging, but this was bad news for British Rail. Hundreds of trains were cancelled because it was the 'wrong type of snow' - a type which blew into the smallest crevice. For three weeks, the rail service was thrown into chaos and even when the snow melted by the third week, only half the scheduled trains ran due to the extent of damage to rolling stock.

A short spell of cold with an inch of snow at Banstead on 9th December gave a hint of what was to follow six weeks after Christmas. On 4th February the temperature dropped below freezing in the afternoon and failed to rise above zero until 11th over a wide area of Surrey. Thursday 7th February was a sensational day, with heavy snow showers and a maximum of just 22F (-5.5C) at Burgh Heath, and 23F (-5C) at Coulsdon and Reigate. This was one of the coldest days of the century in Surrey and certainly the chilliest February day since 1956 when a similar figure was recorded at Gatton Point, Redhill, by the late Mr Christopher Bull.

During the big freeze, about seven inches of snow lay in the northern part of Surrey around Kingston - and almost as much was measured elsewhere. John's Army Surplus Store in Merstham High Street near Redhill reported a huge boom in business, bettering pre-Christmas trading. Co-owner Fred Walton boasted that 300 East German fur hats were sold in two weeks and there was an enormous run on East German border guard officers' great coats. Tank suits and West German parka jackets were sold out and shelves of collapsible shovels were stripped bare. Only a few pairs of German para boots were left out of a large delivery.

More than a hundred seagulls driven inland by the bitter weather in February 1991 descended on the Stamford Green pond at Epsom. But the ice was gaining territory.

In the Ashley Centre, Epsom, Lester Bowden's store sold 400 pairs of Wellingtons in three days and at Dorking, panic buying of food was reported with Waitrose selling out of bread in the middle of the day.

The snowfalls were caused by warmer Mediterranean air pushing north into the bitterly cold airstream. The milder air was sent aloft, causing snow-laden clouds to form. At Coulsdon there was an air frost every night from 1st to 21st.

As the snow swept down on Thursday night, 7th February, a major fire at Belmont School, Holmbury St Mary, lit up the night sky for miles around. The old building, which stands high on the North Downs, was festooned with icicles after firemen hosed down the flames in temperatures around 18F (-8C). Firemen used axes to smash the ice covering a swimming pool so they could draw off a water supply. They also used mallets to smash the ice off snow-covered hydrants. Council lorries had to grit the winding lane up to the school before fire tenders could move in.

Even in town centres earlier that evening the temperature was incredibly low. Reigate shivered at 21F (-6C) during rush hour.

In the small hours of Saturday 9th February another serious fire occurred. Thatched Cottage in Garden Walk at Hooley, went up in flames, and again, water from the firemen's hoses formed icicles inches from the flames. It was a perishingly cold night. A few hours earlier, the temperature at Newlands Corner, Guildford, stood at 21F (-6C) but by 3am it was down to 16F (-9C) at the scene of the blaze. In the nearby Chipstead Valley, the mercury plummeted to 3F (-16C) at dawn.

The weekend of 9th-10th February saw thousands flock to the slopes of Box Hill, Richmond Park and Banstead Woods, wearing dazzling ski costumes as they partook in a variety of winter sports. Some of the younger children had not experienced the delights of snow before. At Box Hill, several excited tobogganers ended up hurt and fifteen were conveyed to hospital by ambulance. People were using anything from canoes to car bonnets and For Sale signs to race downhill much to the alarm of the ambulance crews. One officer said the crazed revellers were 'like lemmings rushing over a cliff.'

Midnight sledging parties were held in Reigate Priory on the Saturday night - the participants carrying small flasks of spirits.

A man clearing snow at St John's School, Leatherhead, died after his exertions and at Epsom, police had to break into homes at Downs Road and Beech Grove where collapsed pensioners were found suffering from the cold. Firemen using turntable ladders hacked down huge icicles overhanging shoppers in Church Street East, Woking. The evening of Tuesday 12th February brought the worst conditions of the cold snap to eastern parts of Surrey. While Kingston had only sleet, several hours of heavy snow fell over Banstead, Reigate and Oxted. Councillor Mrs Diana Bowes from Banstead was one of 30 motorists who had to abandon their cars on Reigate Hill and seek shelter. Gatwick Airport closed for several hours and the M25 between Reigate and Merstham took on the appearance of a snowy farm track.

Mild weather arrived from the west in the last week of February and children watched disappointed as their snowmen drooped, dripped and disappeared.

Banstead High Street on Tuesday, 12th February 1991 - the night thirty cars had to be abandoned above the M25 at Reigate Hill.

Caterham Valley on Thursday 7th February 1991. This was one of the coldest days this century. Warlingham's 'warmest' moment that day was just 22F (-5.5C).

Station Road East, Oxted, also pictured on 7th February 1991.

New Malden fountain on 12th February 1991. The bus to Kingston can be seen in the background.

Bus drivers faced treacherous conditions on the 164 service between Banstead, Sutton and Wimbledon in February 1991.

Woodcote Village near Purley - bleak and icy after the heavy snow on the night of Tuesday 12th February 1991. Nine inches of snow lay on the ground in the higher parts of Croydon by the early hours of Wednesday 13th February, but at Hook near Surbiton, only a light covering was observed.

It's snow joke being a snowman. One minute everything in the garden is lovely with plunging temperatures and a grand easterly wind. The next thing you know, the mercury's risen and a life-threatening south westerly wind has set in. Never mind, Fred the snowman of Burney Road, Westhumble, has been immortalised on this page after his brief but short life in February 1991 outside the home of Ann Cattermole.

When the going gets tough, mountain bikes are what you need. This was the scene at Addiscombe, Croydon, on 1st August 1991 captured by a Croydon Advertiser photographer after a localised thunderstorm.

Summer Arrives Late

1991

When warm, moist air is allowed to rise to great heights the stage is set for dramatic weather. A sure sign that something is about to happen is when clouds tower like vast mountain ranges in the early morning sky.

To the north, east and west, Croydon was virtually hemmed in by thunder clouds mid-morning on 1st August 1991. During the afternoon a violent thunderstorm broke over the town. At first, the thunder was somewhat distant but it steadily increased in ferocity as the skies darkened and torrents of rain fell. In the offices of Kerr Oratis, Accountants, in Shirley, staff moved away from windows as hail beat against the glass. At the rear, water had gathered like a small lake and poured in.

Shops in Lower Addiscombe Road were awash as the sudden downpour proved too much for drains. At Thornton Heath, the Seeboard Showrooms near the Clock Tower saw a mini-tidal wave surge in through the front door and out the rear doors. But close by at Coulsdon, the ground was bone dry.

Guildford, too, had a sudden and violent thunderstorm and in North Street, water split road surfaces as storm drains were unable to cope. Marble-sized hail accompanied the storm. One shop, Book Ends, lost thousands of volumes as power failed and filthy water poured in. Debenham's had to close its protective doors to keep out floodwater, and the fire brigade had a busy time pumping out.

Guildford had already suffered a lively storm during the late evening of Friday, 5th July. A house in Envis Way on the Fairlands estate near Worplesdon was struck by lightning and a roof blaze ensued. One person was treated for shock.

Both June and July were very unsettled, but August brought a complete change. Only four days saw any measurable rain and apart from the extreme heat of 1990 it was the warmest August since 1976.

Summer reached its peak on 1st September when parts of Surrey had their warmest day of the year, the first time September can boast this distinction since 1954.

Postscript . . .

SHOWERS OF CRABS AND FROGS

On 19th July 1829 a violent thunderstorm beset the House of Industry at Redhill.

The fall of water was so great as to appear like an inundation. After the floods had subsided, four crabs were found alive and moving. The species was the common crab.

A few years previous at this location, after a severe downfall of rain, the ground was positively covered with thousands of toads and frogs and many were lodged on roofs of some of the houses.

About the Authors

Mark Davison has always shown a keen interest in the weather.

As a child, he could not be persuaded to come indoors out of the snow. And when, as a teenager, the great storm hit Hook in 1973 he was reprimanded by his parents for going off in search of news stories rather than helping them mop up their flooded home.

After leaving school in Kingston, he joined the Kingston Borough News just in time to cover the 1976 drought stories.

Later, he joined the Surrey Mirror Series at Redhill, working for a time on the Banstead Herald at Epsom, before moving to the Caterham Times at Oxted.

Now he is deputy editor of the Surrey Mirror at Reigate, the town where he lives.

Mark also has a keen interest in live music and runs a weekly column giving news of local bands.

For a number of years he compiled a local history page in his local newspaper which is still a popular feature today. Many of the elderly people he has interviewed as part of his job have supplied anecdotes and photographs for this book.

The ever changing moods and patterns of our skies have always fascinated Ian Currie (right) and the spectacular thunderstorm of September 1958 and the prolonged deep winter snows of 1962-1963 were childhood memories that have never faded. Indeed his first weather station, a Christmas present, had only just been set up when it was almost buried by a heavy snowfall on Boxing Day 1962.

Sharing his interest with others has been a feature of Ian's life. He writes a weekly weather column for the Surrey Mirror, Sutton Herald and Surrey Comet news groups as well as having a regular slot on United Artists Cable Television, Radio Redhill and now Radio Mercury.

A graduate in Geography and Earth Science, he is also a full time teacher, organises field courses and talks to local groups and societies. He re-established the meteorological section of Croydon Natural History and Scientific Society in Croydon, is a member of the Climatological Observers Link and a Fellow of the Royal Meteorological Society.

Along with Mark Davison he has written 'Surrey in the Hurricane' and 'London's Hurricane'. He is married with two boys and lives in Coulsdon.